CAMBRIDGE SKILLS FOR FLUENCY
Series Editor: Adrian Doff

Writing 3

Andrew Littlejohn

CAMBRIDGE
UNIVERSITY PRESS

Published by the Press Syndicate of the University of Cambridge
The Pitt Building, Trumpington Street, Cambridge CB2 1RP
40 West 20th Street, New York, NY 10011–4211, USA
10 Stamford Road, Oakleigh, Melbourne 3166, Australia

© Cambridge University Press 1993

First published 1993

Printed in Great Britain
by Scotprint Ltd, Musselburgh, Scotland

ISBN 0 521 39927 0

w v

Contents

Map of the book

Thanks

Many thanks to:

Alison Silver, Lindsay White and Amanda Ogden at Cambridge University Press for making the book possible;

Adrian Doff and the numerous anonymous reviewers whose comments led to many improvements;

Diana Hicks for energy and inspiration;

and, most important of all, Lita, Daniel and Fiona for their unfailing patience and support.

The author and publishers would also like to thank the following teachers and institutions, where *Writing 3* was piloted, for all their detailed comments and constructive suggestions:

Miles Craven, Eurocentre, Cambridge; Dominic Fisher, Filton Technical College, Bristol; Marie Louise Grogan, English Language Centre, Hove; Norma Innes, Lilliput English Centre, Bournemouth; Sean Power, ASC Language Training, Geneva; Heather Weyh, KONE Hannover; Pamela Murphy, Godmer House, Oxford; John Fields and Carol Hunter.

Introduction to students

Writing 3 contains many different activities to help you learn English. The book has two main aims: to help you develop your ability to write in English and, at the same time, to help you develop your general abilities in English, through writing.

The book is full of choices. You can do the units in any order and, in most cases, you don't have to do everything in each one. Some of the units in the book are linked to each other (see, for example, Units 9 and 10). These develop a topic over two units although, with the exception of Units 17 and 18, 19 and 20, they may each be done independently. The book as a whole covers many different aspects of learning English and of writing in English. If there is a particular thing that you want to practise or learn about, look at the *Map of the book* on pages iv–v. That will tell you which unit it is in.

For many activities, you have to work *with* someone. Sometimes you will write something in a small group and then exchange with other students (each person in the group should write – not just one person). Sometimes you will write something by yourself and then compare it with your neighbour. The point of this is not just to write, but to *talk* about writing. In this way, you will improve not only your writing but your general knowledge of English as well.

Some of the exercises in the book tell you to look at an activity card at the back of the book. This will give you some information or help you write. It is very important that, when you look at your activity card, you only look at *your* card. Don't look at the cards intended for other groups of students – it will spoil the fun!

We hope you learn a lot from this book and enjoy using it.

1 | First impressions

This unit concerns the impressions we form of people. It includes ways of describing the character and appearance of a person and shows you how to write a description of someone. It also focusses on what influences the impressions we form of people.

1   Even when we do not know people well, we usually form an impression of them. Try an experiment. Write your name on a piece of paper, and put it in a pile with everyone else's names. Take a name and look at that person for a minute or two (not too obviously!). Note down your impressions about each of these points:

where he/she grew up   his/her job
what his/her living room looks like   his/her favourite food
his/her taste in music   the car he/she drives (if any)
his/her taste in reading   other interests he/she has

Fold the paper and write the person's name on the front. Then give each paper to the appropriate person. Read the paper about you. How accurate is it? Tell the rest of the class what is right and what is wrong.

2   We also form impressions from someone's appearance. Look at the photographs opposite and note down in a few words your immediate impressions of each person. For example:

Photo 1: a bit scruffy, untidy, very informal. Looks friendly and cheerful – a student? lives in flat or house with similar people (the house is a mess!). 22/23 years old? lots of friends, travels a lot and goes out a lot. Looks musical or artistic – she's probably very talkative!

Some useful words:

smart   efficient   mischievous   elegant
thoughtful   untidy   melancholy   gentle
cheeky   easygoing   neat   unkempt
grubby   eccentric   good-humoured   business-like

**When you are ready, compare your notes with your neighbour's.
Discuss why you formed these impressions.**

**Now, as a class, make a list of some of the different words you used to
describe the people in the photographs. Divide your list into two categories:**
appearance **and** *character*.

Appearance	Character
scruffy	friendly
untidy	cheerful
very informal	artistic
	talkative

3

3 Look back at the photographs and your list of words. Choose one photograph and see if there are any more words you can add to your description of that person. Then, using your imagination, note down your answers to these questions about the person you chose.

What is his/her name?
Where was he/she born?
Where does he/she live now?
What type of house does he/she live in?
What does he/she do?
What is he/she good at?

What does he/she like doing?
How does he/she feel about him/herself?
Is he/she a happy person?
Where is he/she right now? Why?
Where is he/she going next?
Who will be there?

Now, using your answers to some of the questions and your notes from Exercise 2, write a description of the person you chose. For example:

Emma was born in a small town in the south of England. She comes from a happy family, and is the eldest of four daughters. She lived at home until she became a student, which is what she is now. She is an amiable, cheerful person who makes friends easily. She is very talented musically and can play several instruments, including the violin, piano, guitar and different recorders. Right now, Emma is...

Exchange papers with your neighbour. Can you help each other to improve your work? Think about the words that you used and the way you phrased each sentence, as well as grammar, spelling and punctuation.

If your neighbour chose the same person as you, how similar are the descriptions you each wrote?

EXTENSION

4 We also form impressions of people from the facts that we hear about them. Work in a small group. Choose one person from A, B or C opposite and turn to the activity card at the back of the book. Then, in your group, decide on precise details about that person. For example, if the information on the card says the person is 'interested in sports', you could note down the following:

Sports – likes playing football with friends from work and watching it on TV. He goes to football matches whenever he can.

For person A, see activity card 6.
For person B, see activity card 20. *Only look at your group's card!*
For person C, see activity card 28.

When you have discussed all the points, write a description of the person's lifestyle. Decide who in your group will work on each part. The description should have three parts, each beginning:

A typical working day for *(name)* begins at . . . *say what happens.*
After work, *(name)* likes to relax by . . . *say what he/she does.*
At the weekend, *(name)* . . . *say what he/she does.*

While you are writing, help each other with grammar, spelling, phrasing and so on.

When you are ready, compare what you have written with a group who wrote about another person. How different are the people that you described?

Finally, look at the information that each group had. What differences were there in the information? Which piece of information most influenced their description?

2 | Dear friend

This unit is about writing informal letters to friends or acquaintances. It shows you how to write a short letter and gives you the opportunity to get a reply from someone in your class.

1 **Here are some short letters between friends or acquaintances. What would you say is the main reason for writing each letter?**

Contra Porti 33,
Vicenza 36100,
Italy

16th March

Dear Jim and Phyl,
 This is just to let you know that I got back home safely and to say thanks for the weekend. I really enjoyed it. You really must come and visit me sometime soon.

 I've ordered those things you asked for and I'll post them as soon as they arrive.

 Thanks again – love to Caroline.
 Much love,
 Flavia

P.S. The things came to about Lit. 130,000.

45 The Crescent
Worcester WR5 3FG
Tel 0905 557849

3 Sept

Dear Susi,
Congratulations! I've just heard the news about your promotion – Area Manager! I bet you're delighted – will this mean that you won't have to travel so much now? Well done.

I was looking for my French language book the other day. Do you still have it? I can't remember who I gave it to and I've promised it to another friend. It's got a blue cover with a picture of Paris on it. I think it's called France Extra, or something. If you do have it and you don't need it any more, could you let me have it back? Thanks.

Anyway, good luck in your new job. I'll try to come and see you later on when you've had a chance to settle down.

Best wishes and take care of yourself,
 Anne

55 Garner Rd
Cardiff
CF4 6LA

0222 874513
14 June

Dear Bertil,

Here's the cheque for the jumper. I've made it out to you – is that all right? I just hope that it hasn't been sold – don't forget: size 12 and I wanted the one with blue and yellow in it. I've added £3 to the cheque to cover the postage.

Hoping that you are keeping well,

Love Helen.
xxx

Nordhemsgatan 44A
41306 Göteborg
Sweden
20 March

Dear Ray,

I thought I'd just drop you a line to say that I've got my tickets and I have checked the train times from the airport. I am arriving at Exeter at about 4.30 on Saturday (21st) but please don't worry about meeting me at the station – I can take a taxi up to your house. The train will probably be late anyway!

Until then,
Regards
Lasse

Look at the letters again and complete a letter outline like the one below with examples of what you can say to open a letter and to close it. Add any other phrases you can think of.

My address

Date

Dear...

Opening:

Message

Closing:

Name

2

Choose one of the situations below and write a short letter. Decide what information you need to give (you can invent any details you require). You may find it useful to refer to the letters in Exercise 1 for help or ideas.

A You are going on holiday to Australia. A friend who you haven't seen for a long time lives there. Write and tell him or her that you are coming and that you will get in touch when you arrive so that perhaps you can meet. (Say when you are coming, where you will stay and how long for.)

> Dear...
> How are you? We
> haven't seen each
> other for ages.
> Well,...

B You and some friends want to rent a cottage in the mountains for a week but you need more people to join the group. Write to some other friends asking them if they want to come. (Say when you are going, where to and how much it will cost.)

> Dear...
> How would you like to
> spend a week in the
> mountains?

C Some friends of a friend are coming to live in your area. You are sending them some leaflets about your town. Briefly tell them what it is like living there and say that you hope that they will get in touch with you when they arrive.

> Dear...
> George tells me
> that...

D Some friends came to stay with you last week and you have just found a pair of socks and a left shoe under their bed. You think (but you are not sure) that the things belong to them. Also, you have lost a jumper and you think that they might have taken it by mistake. Write and ask them. (Describe the shoe and socks and your jumper.)

> Dear...
> This is just a
> note to ask...

If you would like help while you are writing, show your letter to the person next to you. See if he or she can suggest any ways to improve what you have written.

When you have finished, give your completed letter to another student. Write a short reply to the letter you receive:

If you get a situation A letter, see activity card 14.
If you get a situation B letter, see activity card 27.
If you get a situation C letter, see activity card 8.
If you get a situation D letter, see activity card 22.

(If you prefer, you can invent your own reply.)

EXTENSION

3 Imagine that you want to write to a friend or acquaintance to let them know how you are and what you have been doing recently. Think first about the most important aspects of your life at the moment and make some notes under each one, like this:

House
decorating the
kitchen

Family
Louis' new job

Work
too much!
two new bosses

English
started a new course
twice a week

Holidays
off to the United States in
the summer (California to
visit Ed and Lynne)

Now, use your notes to help you write your letter. You could begin by saying first what you are doing now:

Dear...
I'm sitting here in my English lesson and I thought I'd write to let you know how I am. Everybody is busy writing so it's quite quiet.

Then use your notes to form separate paragraphs in your letter:

Everything is fine at the moment. Work is going quite well but, as usual, there's too much to do every day and I end up taking work home. But it's all very enjoyable. We've got two new bosses. They seem all right but it is difficult to know how they will be later on.
Louis has just started a new job, by the way. He's got a job in the administration department at the hospital. He says it's OK, though a little boring. ...

You could perhaps finish by giving an excuse for ending the letter, like this:

Anyway, I had better stop now. I've run out of time and I have to make sure I don't miss the bus home.

Let me know how you are,
Best wishes,
Chantal

4 When you have finished, pass your letter to someone in your class. Read the letter that you are given and write a short reply. You can make comments or ask questions about anything in the letter. For example:

It was interesting to hear about Louis' job. My sister, Josie, works in the administration department at the hospital. She works mostly at night, bringing medical records up to date. Perhaps they know each other?

3 | Through a window

This unit asks you to imagine that you are looking into a room through a window and to write a description of what you can see. The unit then offers you the opportunity to exchange texts with another student in order to help you develop your ideas further.

1 Here are some photographs of rooms in various parts of the world. How would you describe them?

Note down under three headings the different words you could use. For example:

Room	Size and shape	Light	Overall impression
a)	Large	bright	cold sterile
	rectangular	harsh	stark

Some useful words:

spacious   roomy   tiny   rectangular   square   round   dark
dim   gloomy   sombre   airy   crowded   comfortable   threatening
welcoming   relaxing   peaceful   elegant   luxurious

Compare your impressions with other people in your class. What about the room you are in now? How would you describe that?

2   Here are some pictures of windows. Which country do you think they are in? What makes you think that? What does the rest of each building look like, do you think?

Look at one of the windows again and imagine the room behind it. Note down your answers to these questions:

What does the room look like?
What objects are there in the room? Can you describe them?
There is someone in the room. Who is it? What is he or she doing and thinking?
What sounds and smells are there? Where are they coming from?

Now, using your notes, write about the room. Leave lots of space so that you can make changes and add points later. For example:

— dark inside
— an old bed, table, bowl and jug of water. There's a photo on the wall: a wedding couple?
— damp
— an old Lady doing some embroidery
— there's the sound of a child crying somewhere in the distance

The room is rather dark and there's a strong smell of damp. It's cold in the room, despite the bright sunshine outside. In the corner, there is a small table with a china bowl and a jug full of water. Just above it, on the wall, there is a faded photograph of a wedding couple. The man is tall and handsome and the woman has a long flowing dress. Near the window, an old lady sits...

While you are writing, ask other students or the teacher for help with spelling, grammar, phrasing and so on.

3 **When you are ready, exchange papers with another student. Carefully read through the paragraph you receive and, on the back of the paper, add some questions concerning the things which you would like to know more about. For example:**

Is there anything else on the wall?
When was the photograph taken, do you think? Does the picture only show the wedding couple?
Tell me more about the old lady. What does she look like?

13

When you get your paper back, see if you can add answers to some of the questions. For example:

The room is rather dark and there's a strong smell of damp. It's cold in the room, despite the bright sunshine outside. In the corner, there is a small table with a china bowl and a jug full of water. Just above it, on the wall, there is a faded photograph of a wedding couple, taken perhaps in the 1920s or 30s. The man is tall and handsome and the woman has a long flowing dress. Near the window, an old lady sits... They are in another country, surrounded by palm trees and beautiful flowers. Other than the photograph, the walls are bare.

Pass your paper around the class for other people to read or, alternatively, read your paper out to the rest of the class. Can you guess which window other people were looking through?

EXTENSION

4 Read through your paper again or, if you prefer, exchange with another student. Imagine that, suddenly, something happens. There is a noise, outside or inside the room. What is it? What does the person in the room do? What happens next? Add a paragraph to the description of the room (either your own description or another student's).

Suddenly, ...

5 Work in small groups. Read through each other's work. Talk first about the part after 'suddenly' and how the description ends. Did you expect that ending?

Next, see if you can suggest ways to improve what you have each written. Think about:

The words used – can you suggest alternative words which create a stronger impression?

The way the description 'flows' – would it sound better if some sentences were added or taken out? Which?

Points of grammar, spelling and punctuation – can you suggest changes which make the meaning clearer?

4 | Assessing your writing abilities

When you are learning something, it is often useful to think about what you already know as this can help you see what you need to learn. This unit asks you to consider what you are able to do in writing in English. It shows you how to design some exercises and offers you a choice of exercises designed by other students. You can also begin a diary of your progress in English.

1 What are you *personally* able to do in writing in English? Think about the different types of writing that you can do. For example, write a business letter, a recipe, a description, and so on. Look through *Writing 3* and your other coursebooks for ideas.

Then, working in a small group, write down the things that each person mentions. Try to be as specific as possible. For example:

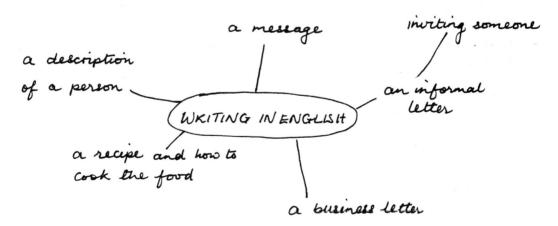

Join another group and compare your ideas. Do you want to add anything else to your notes?

2   Look at your notes again and for each type of writing show *how well* you think you can do it. Write *very well, quite well, not very well* or *not at all* beside each point.

Now, with another student, choose two or three types of writing which you feel you are good at and, for each one, design a task to practise it. (Use a separate piece of paper for each one.) Give precise instructions of what to write and sign it. For example:

Write a letter

You are going on holiday to the United States. You want to book hotel rooms in New York for three nights for yourself and your two travelling companions. Write a letter to book the rooms.

                                Cristina and Mitsuko

Write a message

You are in a town where some old friends live. You haven't seen them for a long time. You go to their house but they are out. Write a message to put through their letter box.

                                Cristina and Mitsuko

3   When everyone in the class is ready, place all the tasks together. Choose one of the tasks, either to test yourself or to practise something you feel you are not very good at. Check how you rated your abilities in Exercise 2 and then try to do the task. Was your estimate correct?

Ask the teacher, the students who designed the task, or your neighbour to look at what you have written. Can you or they see any ways to improve your work? (Think about the words you use, the style and how clear the meaning is, as well as grammar, spelling and punctuation.)

What about the tasks themselves? Can you see any ways to improve them?

EXTENSION

4   Think about other aspects of your English. What do you do to get practice? Where do you feel you need more practice? Write a diary of what you have done in English this week and say how easy or difficult you found it. Decide what you will do in the next week to improve your English further. For example:

3 – 10th February

Reading   I read an article about Africa in Newsweek. It was quite difficult, but I learnt a lot of new words.

Listening   I tried to listen to an English language radio station but they seemed to speak very fast. Perhaps I just have to get used to their way of speaking. I'll try again tonight.

Writing   I started a letter to Peter, but didn't finish. It's very hard work!

Speaking   I didn't do anything in particular.

Overall: The thing I need most at the moment, I think, is to increase my vocabulary and to improve my pronunciation.

ACTION
• buy an English newspaper or magazine to read on the bus
• buy a good dictionary and carry a notebook
• record myself speaking English on a cassette player and try to improve my pronunciation

If you write a new diary entry every week or two, you can see your improvement over time.

5 | Poet's corner

Trying to write poetry in a foreign language can be a useful and interesting experience, even if you rarely write or read poetry in your own language. By trying to write poems you can learn about the effects of particular words. This unit includes some different types of poetry that you can experiment with.

1 A very simple type of poem (called an acrostic) uses letters of a word or of the alphabet to start each line or spell a word. Here are some examples. How does the writer of each one feel?

> Tired, longing for a bed
> Reading, trying to kill the time
> Aching legs, no room to stretch
> Visits to distant friends, *when* will we arrive?
> Empty seats to slump across
> Loathing the return

> Another afternoon of celebration
> Black clouds gather beyond
> Coats and capes hurry past my window
> Dogs stand huddled against the wall
> Electric storms are threatening
> Far away they rumble
> Gutters splashing, overflowing
> Humbled, good to be alive

> *Where have the yea*R*s gone?*
> *Our arms* E*mbrace*
> *Changes* U*nseen*
> *Sorrows* N*ot known*
> *Ghosts of the past w*I*thin*
> L*O*st friend,*
> *Where have the years go*N*e?*

Choose a topic and try to write an acrostic. (Use a dictionary to help you to find words to start each line.) Here are some ideas:

summer	the sea	the wind	work	childhood	old age
home	nature	an animal	waking up	winter	family life
peace	sunshine	being alone	a particular person		

2 Another simple form of poem is the Japanese 'haiku' which, although very short, can often create a strong atmosphere. A haiku usually has a particular structure, with only three lines.

The first line has five syllables: *Furu ike ya*   An old pond
The second line has seven syllables: *Kawazu tobikomu* A frog jumps—
The third line has five syllables: *Mizu no oto*   Sound of water
                 Basho (1644–94)

The haiku form has been used by many English poets as well, often with a slight variation. How many of these examples follow the structure exactly?

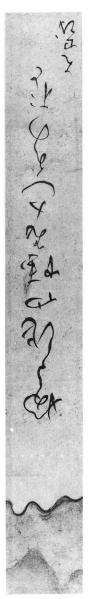

Young men are fools
and now I am old
I am a fool.
   C. H. Sisson

Summer Haiku

Silence
and deeper silence
as the crickets hesitate.
   Leonard Cohen

Two Haiku

only trouble with
Japanese haiku is that
you write one, and then

only seventeen
syllables later you want
to write another.
   Roger McGough

3 Choose a topic (see the list in Exercise 1 for ideas) and try to write your own haiku. First, collect your ideas and impressions about the topic. This, for example, is the beginning of a haiku on *Winter*.

Winter
trees bare   draughts through the window
ice   crisp morning air   wind
cold kitchen and hall floors
in the car
      keeping doors closed: heating bills!
              Staying at home — longing for the sun!
heavy blankets on the bed
      pains in my feet

Next, look at your ideas and decide which ones you would like to develop. Don't worry about syllable length at first – concentrate on developing your ideas.

Winter

Coming downstairs — ??   4
my foot on the ~~bare~~ hall floor ~~to~~ 7
~~I can feel the~~ sharp ~~pain~~ of ~~the night~~ frost
                    ness   the

Then, as your ideas become clearer, try to build them into a haiku. Keep reading your words aloud quietly and make changes to get more or less the right number of syllables in each line.

Cold ~~bitter~~ mornings   bones?
~~Out from my warm bed~~ cold inside my bones
my foot on the bare hall floor   7
    sharpness of the ~~night~~ frost   5

Cold inside ~~my~~ bones   ?   morning?
my foot on the bare hall floor
    sharpness of the frost

Here, for example, are the changes the writer of 'Winter' made before arriving at a 'finished' version.

Winter
A ~~crisp~~ Cold morning air   waking?
    my foot on ~~the~~ bare hall floor
                    a
sharpness of ~~the~~ frost
              a

                breathing
Waking, ~~to the~~ cold
      my foot on a bare hall floor
      sharpness of a frost

When you have finished, read your haiku aloud to other students.

WINTER

WAKING, BREATHING COLD

   MY FOOT ON A BARE HALL FLOOR

     SHARPNESS OF A FROST

EXTENSION

4   Here are some more poems. Choose the one that you like most and try to write a similar poem yourself. Copy the first two or three lines, close the book and continue in your own way. (Alternatively, write a completely different poem. The list of topics in Exercise 1 may give you some ideas.)

Silence

I spoke, but no one heard.
I listened, and heard nothing.
People moved past me
Silently.
I drank, and the water made no sound
   in its glass.
I ran, and could not hear my feet
   against the ground.
Birds flew and
   perched in their trees
Silently.

The streets were crowded;
Buses, cars, cycles moved
Silently.
The hands of the clocks
   reached the hour,
But no clock struck.
The wind moved the leaves,
But the trees were silent.
Sound, noises, voices did not exist.

Pamela Coombs

Days that the wind takes over

Days that the wind takes over
Blowing through the gardens
Blowing birds out of the street trees
Blowing cats around corners
Blowing my hair out
Blowing my heart apart
Blowing high in my head
Like the sea sound caught in a shell.
One child put her thin arms around the wind
And they went off together.
Later the wind came back
Alone.

Karla Kuskin

⟫→

Lazy man's song

I could have a job, but am too lazy to choose it;
I have got land, but am too lazy to farm it.
My house leaks; I am too lazy to mend it.
My clothes are torn; I am too lazy to darn them.
I have got wine, but I am too lazy to drink it;
So it's just the same as if my cup were empty.
I have got a lute, but I am too lazy to play;
So it's just the same as if it had no strings.
My family tells me there is no more steamed rice;
I want to cook, but I am too lazy to grind.
My friends and relatives write me long letters;
I should like to read them, but they're such a bother to open.
I have always been told that Hsi Shu-yeh
Passed his whole life in absolute idleness.
But he played his lute and sometimes worked at his forge;
So even *he* was not so lazy as I.

Po Chu-i, AD811, translated by Arthur Waley

Leisure

What is this life if, full of care,
We have no time to stand and stare.

No time to stand beneath the boughs
And stare as long as sheep or cows.

No time to see, when woods we pass,
Where squirrels hide their nuts in grass.

No time to turn at Beauty's glance,
And watch her feet, how they dance.

No time to wait till her mouth can
Enrich that smile her eyes began.

A poor life this if, full of care,
We have no time to stand and stare.

W. H. Davies

6 | Circular stories

Circular stories begin and end with the same sentence. In this unit you can write a short circular story that starts and ends with a description of something happening. The unit includes an example of a story with an air of mystery.

1 **Work in small groups. Choose a time and a place from the boxes below and then imagine a scene in that place at that time. What can you see? What sounds or smells are there? What is the atmosphere like? Make a list of the different points that each person in your group mentions.**

When?

early in the morning, before sunrise   at dawn just before breakfast
lunch time   the middle of the afternoon   the early evening
dusk   at night

Where?

in a train   in a plane   on a boat   in a hot air balloon
in a city centre   in a public park   on a beach   in the country
in a forest   up a mountain

For example:

<u>Dawn in the country</u>

sun just rising   dew – wet grass
pink skies   wet trouser legs as you walk
very quiet, peaceful   an owl, a cockerel
cold   road 'crunches' as you walk
a thin mist   you can see your breath

23

2

Working first in your group, think of a person in the place and at the time
you chose. Decide if the person is male or female, how old he or she is and
what he or she is doing. For example:

walking to catch a bus	reading a book or newspaper
just about to sit down to eat	sleeping
talking to someone	relaxing
sitting down, crying into his or her hands	driving

Next, by yourself, give the person a name and describe the scene in detail.
What *precisely* was he or she doing? What could the person see, feel or hear?
What was he or she thinking about? What other things were happening at
the same time? Write down your ideas in the form of a story. Look back at
your notes from Exercise 1 as you write.

   Here, for example, a middle-aged man is walking to catch a bus in the
country at dawn.

Jack Riley pulled on his boots and opened the door of
his cottage. Outside, dawn was just beginning and a thin
mist covered the fields. He closed the door gently behind
him, picked up his bag of tools and walked down the
small country road, whistling as he went. A loud noise
startled him and, looking back, he could see a woman
climbing onto a tractor. It was just another working day.

   As he turned the corner to the main road, a
rabbit ran across his path. He smiled to himself.
In front of him, the sky was turning bright pink. Long,
thin clouds floated across the sun. Riley was happy,
things were going very well for him now. He joined the
main road and stood waiting for the first bus of the day.

While you are writing, discuss your story with the people in your group.
Show them your work and see if they can suggest further ideas for you to
include.

3

Suddenly . . .
And then what happened? Add a sentence or two to describe something that
dramatically changed the situation.

Suddenly, as if from nowhere, a young man appeared
from the woods behind him. He was screaming something
and running straight at Riley.

Now exchange papers with someone in your group (or, if you prefer,
continue the story yourself). Read through the story so far and think about
what happened next – how did the situation develop?

"I know!" he screamed, "I know!" Riley stood still, unaffected. He had
never seen this man before.
"I know!" he screamed again. "I'll tell!"
"What do you want?" asked Riley.
"Five thousand."
Riley stood for a moment and thought. "I'll be late, but it won't
take long."
"Five thousand, and you won't tell?" he said.
"Five thousand, and I won't tell."
"Come with me."
The young man followed Riley up the lane to his cottage.
"Come in," said Riley, "It won't take long." He closed the door
behind them and turned the key.

4   To end the story, you have to return to your opening sentence. If you
exchanged stories with another student, get your story back. Read through
your story again and look back at your notes from Exercise 1 so you can
continue to develop the atmosphere. You may need to make changes to the
story so that the end closes the circle.

The young man followed Riley up the lane to his cottage.
                      checking that no one had seen the young man enter, he
"Come in," said Riley, "It won't take long." He/closed the door

behind them and turned the key.
       A short time later
       In the distance, Riley heard the bus pass on the main road.
"Still time to get the next one," he thought. Jack Riley pulled
on his boots and opened the door of his cottage.

When you are ready, exchange your completed stories with students in other
groups. Can you suggest ways to improve the stories? (Think about the
words that are used and the impressions that they give, as well as grammar,
spelling and punctuation.)

⋙→

EXTENSION

5 **Read through your story again and see if you can develop it further. For example, you could do one of the following:**

- Include one or two more people, animals or important objects in it.
- Add or remove parts to strengthen the atmosphere. (Can you make it more forceful by saying less? Can you make it more vivid by giving greater detail?)
- Include more dialogue to give a feeling of action.
- Say what each person was thinking. (Give the actual words that were in their head.)
- Describe more clearly *how* each person did something.

7 | What makes a good piece of writing?

This unit concerns the characteristics of a good piece of writing. You will need to have some of your previous pieces of writing available so that you can look back at them. The unit helps you to identify some ways of improving your writing and to make a list of the mistakes you often make.

1 What makes a good piece of writing? Think of the stories, newspaper articles, letters and so on that you have read (in English or in your own language). What characteristics did the well-written ones have? What did the badly-written ones lack? Work in a small group and add further characteristics to the picture below. Try to be as specific as possible.

Share your ideas with the rest of the class. Add to the picture any further characteristics that other people mention.

In *your* writing in English, which characteristics do you think are most important? Why?

2

Read through the examples below and discuss each one with your neighbour. Do you feel that they are good pieces of writing? Why/why not? Talk about your answers to these questions:

What is the purpose of the text?   Does it achieve that purpose?
Is it clear and easy to understand?   Are headings used appropriately?
Do some sentences or paragraphs need to be broken down or combined?
Does anything need to be added to, or taken away from, the text?
Does the text need to be reorganised in some way?
Is the grammar, spelling, punctuation and choice of words correct?

Together, write an improved version where you think it is necessary.

Brittany Ferries brochure

From the moment you step on board you'll be in the hands of our Captains – highly trained and respected and delighted to be taking people, in such comfort and safety, to holiday in the country that they are so proud of.

Our technology on board is considered to lead the way and our safety standards – including having fully trained medical staff on board at all times, are second to none.

Or perhaps our croissants, which like all of our baguettes, patisseries and such like we bake fresh each day on board.

Our chefs wouldn't dream of offering anything less. Anymore than our wine stewards would think of offering you anything but first class wine or our information girls be less than friendly and helpful. And our Duty Free shops are stacked high with irresistible bargains, many direct from France itself.

We've paid attention to every detail.

British Rail leaflet

INTERCITY

Seat Reservations

You can normally reserve from 2 months in advance of the day of travel and in most cases you may make a reservation up to 2 hours before the train leaves its first station, or for early-morning trains up to the previous evening.

We advise customers that it is essential to reserve seats on certain services during peak periods. On trains marked ▣ in the timetable pages reservations are ESSENTIAL and free of charge to ticket holders. Those trains marked ▣ will be busy and we strongly RECOMMEND that you reserve seats.

Packing for a child's toy

ECHO MIC

"THE PLAYS WITH IT IN THE FOLLOWING WAYS":

IT DOES NOT USE BATTERY, IT IS OPERATED WITH ECHO. A Super-light megaphone with a lot of enjoyments Such "ECHO MIC" needs not to use the power source which the real megaphone requires, not it uses loud speaker and amplifier etc. With it, we can easily have good time with the interesting megaphone with echo.

"WE CAN PLAY WITH ITS ECHO."
One's mouth makes close to its main body for speaking loudly or singing songs. The skill for one is to speak loudly and then the better echo we can have.

• Ha! Ha! Ha: The drama sepeech on the stage as real as possible.

Notice outside an Immigration Office

ATTENTION

THOSE, WHO NOT DECENTLY DRESSED, WEARING JUST A SLEEVE-LESS SINGLET, WEARING RUBBER FOAM SANDAL OR DRESSING IN HIPPY-LIKE STYLE, LOOKING DIRTY AND NOT TIDIED AND LOOKED ODIOUS TO ANYONE WHO SIGHTS IT, ARE NOT BE ALLOWED TO CONTACT WITH THE IMMIGRATION AUTHORITIES.

Compare the changes you made with those made by other students. Are there any more characteristics that you can add to your notes from Exercise 1?

3   Now look back at the pieces of writing that you have done recently, either at home or in class. Look carefully at each one. Can you see any ways in which they can be improved? Check each piece of writing against your notes from Exercise 1.

  If you would like to, discuss your work with another student. Can he or she suggest any improvements?

EXTENSION

4   One immediate way to improve your writing is to check for mistakes or 'slips of the pen'. Here are some common mistakes in English. Discuss with your neighbour the type of mistake which has been made. Can you correct each one?

a) Normaly, I don't think much about money.
b) What's this.
c) Those shoes aren't enough big for me.
d) Steve works in a restaurant. He's the head cooker.
e) I am a secretary for 6 years.
f) Young people are interested computers.
g) She went into town and she posted the letter and she came back.
h) The car hitted the tree.
i) They has got two horses.
j) I look forward to hearing from you as soon as possible.
k) A fire has destroyed our stocks and therefore that there will be a delay.

5   Look again at your recent pieces of writing. What mistakes do you commonly make? Make a list and try to form a mnemonic of the things to check in your work in future.

ESSIDIP

E in front of s (e.g. ~~x~~spontaneous)
Shorter sentences (fewer relative clauses)
Spelling
Infinitive (e.g. I could talk~~xx~~ to her)
Double letters (e.g. po<u>ss</u>ible)
It (Is <u>it</u> raining?)
Phrasal verbs (e.g. write down, write up, write in)

8 | Seeing what you think

> 'How can I know what I think
> till I see what I say?'
>
> E.M. Forster

Writing is often a useful way of sorting out your ideas about something. This unit presents some techniques for generating ideas, based on ones suggested by the psychologist Edward de Bono. It shows you how you can develop your ideas into a complete text and offers you an opportunity to get feedback on what you have written.

1 First, choose a proposal from the box below or any other proposal which interests you. Alternatively, think about an important decision you have to make, for example, whether you should accept a new job or move to a new house. Think of it as a statement: 'I should accept the job.' 'I should move house.'

Cars should be banned from town centres.	Smoking should be illegal.
Boxing should be banned.	Taxes should be lowered.
All cars should be yellow.	Everyone should wear the same uniform.
Public transport should be free.	There should be no advertising on TV.
Medicines should not be tested on animals.	Seat belts in cars should be compulsory.
All children over 10 should have an afternoon job.	

To begin to discover the main implications of the proposal, use the 'PMI' technique. First, think for a few minutes about the *Plus* points of the proposal, then about the *Minus* points, and finally about points which are just *Interesting* or *Important* in connection with the proposal. Make notes under three separate headings:

PLUS POINTS (P)	MINUS POINTS (M)	INTERESTING POINTS (I)
i.e. what is good about something	*i.e. what is bad about something*	*i.e. other points or points which are neither good nor bad*

For example:

P	M	I

Cars should be banned from town centres.

It would reduce pollution

People wouldn't be able to get to and from work quickly

There's often so much traffic you can't move quickly anyway

2 **Now show your notes to the person next to you and, together, try two further techniques:**

a) **CAF — Consider All Factors**
- Look at the PMI notes you each made. Have you forgotten anything?
- What other things depend on the subject of the proposal? (e.g. What depends on cars?)
- What effect will the proposal have on those other things?
- Can you add more PMI points?

     For example:

P	M	I

Shops would lose a lot of business

Cars take people to shops

Most car accidents happen in towns

Accidents would be reduced

b) **C & S – Consequences and Sequel**
- Look at your Plus and Minus points again. What will happen *as a result of* each point? Think about: (i) immediately, (ii) in a year or two, (iii) in 10–20 years' time.
- Can you add any more PMI points?

     For example:

Cars take people to shops

Shops would lose a lot of business

Most car accidents happen in towns

Accidents would be reduced

Shops would close and many people would lose their jobs

Health costs would fall

The economy of the town would decline

3 Now, by yourself, look back at your notes and try this technique.

FIP – First Important Priorities.
- Which are the most important *Plus* points? Number them 1–3 in order of importance.
- Which are the most important *Minus* points? Number them 1–3 in order of importance.
- Which is the most important point of all? Put an asterisk * by that one.

4 You are now ready to begin writing about your ideas. Look at your notes and decide how you will organise them. There are various possibilities:
- Introduce the topic, then give a plus point, then a minus point, then a plus point, then a minus point and so on until you reach your conclusion.

That usually sounds very broken and makes it difficult to come to a final decision. A better method is probably:
- Introduce the topic, talk about the most important plus points, then the most important minus points and then give your conclusion.

or:
- Introduce the topic, talk about the most important minus points, then the most important plus points and then give your conclusion.

Decide which method you will use and then begin writing about your views. Introduce the topic and then explain each point. After each one, give an example or further details of what you mean. This will help you sharpen your ideas. For example:

<u>Cars should be banned from town centres.</u>

The question of whether cars should be banned or not from town centres is a very complicated one. There are a lot of different factors involved and it is not easy to see which is the best view to take.

In support of the proposal, there are a number of important points. Firstly, banning cars would reduce the amount of pollution in town centres. At the moment, cars produce a lot of exhaust fumes and it is often difficult to breathe. Secondly, ...

Against the proposal, there are a number of other points. Firstly, it would be difficult for people to get to and from work quickly since they would have to wait for buses and taxis. This would not be popular with many people who already work very long days. Secondly,...

Add other points as they occur to you while you are writing. Finally, add a conclusion which gives your overall opinion (look at the point you asterisked).

In conclusion, however, I feel that it is probably a good idea if cars are banned from town centres. Although it will make life more difficult in some respects and may lead to some shops closing down, it will improve the quality of the air and make living and being in the city less dangerous.

Some useful phrases:

Firstly/Secondly/Finally, . . .   In connection with . . .
This is because . . .
Another point in support of/against the proposal is . . .
More importantly, . . .   However, . . .   Although . . . , . . .

Read your work aloud quietly to yourself to see how it sounds and make any changes you feel necessary. Check your work for mistakes that you often make.

5   Exchange papers with another student. Read through his or her paper and then, in your own words, tell your partner what you think he or she is saying. How clearly has your partner expressed his or her meaning?

Together, look carefully at each paper. Can you suggest any ways to improve the way it is written? Think about phrasing, the words used and the examples given, as well as spelling, grammar and punctuation.

EXTENSION

6   The PMI, CAF, C & S and FIP techniques can be used for many different topics. Choose another one from the box in Exercise 1 or think of a proposal of your own and go through the steps in Exercises 1–5. The more you use the techniques, the better you will become at seeing what you think about something.

These thinking tools were designed by Edward de Bono and are copyright material which may not be used without permission. They are taken from the CoRT Thinking programme, which is designed to teach thinking directly as a curriculum subject. The programme is published by Science Research Associates Ltd. Readers are advised to consult that programme for full use of the tools.

9 | Portrait of a nation: Common misconceptions

This unit focusses on the views which other people have of your country and their common misconceptions. Working from notes, you can develop a complete text and get feedback from other students on what you have written.

1 How do people in other countries see your country? What stereotypes do they have? Here, for example, are some typical views which other nationalities have of English people.

Stereotyped views of English people
- a full breakfast of bacon and eggs every morning
- very conservative, reserved, stiff
- live in cold houses (it rains all the time and there is always fog in London)
- the men carry umbrellas and wear bowler hats
- drink tea all day and can't do anything without having a cup of tea first
- eat fish and chips a lot

Think for a few moments and note down the things that other nationalities say are typical of your country.

If there are other students from your country in the class, compare your ideas. If there are students from other countries, show your notes to them and ask them if similar things are said about their country. Is there any truth in these typical views?

2 Look at your notes and think about the discussion in Exercise 1. Select four or five points which you feel are misconceptions about your country and write a short paragraph about each one, describing how things really are. Leave lots of space so that you can make changes later. Here, for example, are some misconceptions about English people.

THE ENGLISH: SOME COMMON MISCONCEPTIONS

1   They eat a full 'English breakfast' every morning.

False. Most English people don't have time in the morning to eat a heavy breakfast, and they would probably not want to. A cup of tea or coffee, a bowl of cereal and a piece of toast is all that most people have. I don't know anyone who eats an 'English breakfast' in the morning.

2   English people live in cold houses.

Partly true. Many English houses have very bad insulation against the cold. Double glazing is still not very common, especially in older houses, and there are often a lot of draughts around doors and windows. As a result, a lot of energy is lost. Modern houses are generally much better insulated, but many visitors still find them cold in the winter.

3 When you have finished, exchange papers with other students. Read through each paper that you receive and add any comments or questions you have. Number each comment or question to show what it refers to and add your name. Like this:

3   The English are very conservative, reserved and stiff.

Partly true. English people are generally fairly quiet and don't get very excited about things. At parties, for example, they often prefer to talk[1] rather than dance. But many of the new and unusual things in music, fashion, comedy and so on have come from England[2].

[1] What do they talk about? Peter

[2] Yes, that's interesting. Can you give some examples? Inge

4 Pass the papers back to the original writers. When you receive your paper,
see if you can put the answers to some of the questions into your work.
When you have finished, show your paper again to the people who wrote the
questions.

3 <u>The English are very conservative, reserved and stiff.</u>

Partly true. English people are generally fairly quiet and don't get very excited about things. At parties, for example, they often prefer to talk (most frequently about their work) rather than dance. But many of the new and unusual things in music, fashion, comedy and so on have come from England. The Beatles, fashion in the "swinging sixties", and Monty Python are all examples of this.

10 | Portrait of a nation: A guide for visitors

This unit asks you to imagine that you have been requested to produce a guide for visitors to your country. It shows you how you can develop your notes into a complete text and then finally present your work as a poster or a leaflet.

1 Imagine that you have been asked to write a profile of your country for visitors. How would you describe life there? Choose three or four of the topics below (or any other areas) and first make some notes about what you think are the most important points.

home life   the media (TV, newspapers)   leisure activities   school   work
social life   childhood   being old   government   politics   food

For example:

Home life

we spend a lot of time at home
heavily furnished houses
decorated walls
a lot of TV
children in bed by 7 or 8 o'clock
    or earlier
small families – 2 or 3 children only

If there are other students from your country in the class, compare your ideas. If there are students from other countries, show your notes to them and ask if there are other points they would like to know more about.

2 Now number each point to show in what order you will write about them.
Add any other points as they occur to you. Like this:

<u>Home life</u>

① we spend a lot of time at home
② heavily furnished houses (+ small rooms, carpets, cold!)
② decorated walls
① a lot of TV
③ children in bed by 7 or 8 o'clock
    or earlier (+ long school day)
③ small families – 2 or 3 children only

(+ people often move away from home when they are about 18 – not just to get married)

3 Using your notes, start writing a draft version of your description. Divide it
into different sections for each topic you made notes about. (If there are
other students from your country in the class, you could take one or two
sections each.)

If you have a lot to say about a topic, divide it into separate paragraphs for each
group of points. This will help to focus the reader's attention. For example:

THE ENGLISH: PORTRAIT OF A NATION

Three aspects: home life, work and social life

Home life

The average English person spends a considerable amount of
time at home, perhaps because the climate in England is
not very reliable. For many people, a lot of this time is
spent watching television. Game shows, quizzes and 'soap
operas' such as Dallas and Neighbours are very popular.
People also occupy themselves by reading, playing games,
listening to music or with various hobbies, such as making
or collecting things. 'DIY' activities, such as redecorating,
renovating furniture and small building projects, are also
very popular.

English homes usually have a lot of furniture in them – armchairs, sofas, bookcases and so on – as well as carpets on the floor and heavy curtains to keep the cold out. Rooms are normally small because they are easier to heat.

An average English family is not very large...

As you write, read through your draft and make changes to ensure that it expresses your meaning clearly. Show your work to the person next to you. Is the meaning clear to them? Do they have any suggestions for improving what you have written?

4 For your final version, decide if you want to present your portrait as a leaflet or a poster. You could include some photographs if you have any and also, if you have done Unit 9, your work on 'common misconceptions', as in the example below.

THE ENGLISH: PORTRAIT OF A NATION

Some common misconceptions

1 They eat a full English breakfast every day
~~~ ~~~ ~~~ ~~~ ~~~ ~~~
~~~ ~~~ ~~~ ~~~ ~~~ ~~~

2 ~~~ ~~~ ~~~ ~~~
~~~ ~~~ ~~~ ~~~ ~~~
~~~ ~~~ ~~~ ~~~
~~~ ~~~ ~~~

3 ~~~ ~~~ ~~~ ~~~
~~~ ~~~ ~~~ ~~~
~~~ ~~~ ~~~ ~~~
~~~ ~~~ ~~~

4 ~~~ ~~~ ~~~ ~~~
~~~ ~~~ ~~~ ~~~
~~~ ~~~ ~~~ ~~~
~~~ ~~~ ~~~ ~~~

5 ~~~ ~~~ ~~~ ~~~
~~~ ~~~ ~~~ ~~~
~~~ ~~~ ~~~ ~~~
~~~ ~~~ ~~~ ~~~

Three aspects of life

Home life
~~~ ~~~ ~~~
~~~ ~~~ ~~~
~~~ ~~~ ~~~
~~~ ~~~ ~~~
~~~ ~~~ ~~~
~~~ ~~~ ~~~
~~~ ~~~ ~~~
~~~ ~~~ ~~~

Work
~~~ ~~~ ~~~ ~~~
~~~ ~~~ ~~~
~~~ ~~~ ~~~
~~~ ~~~ ~~~
~~~ ~~~ ~~~ ~~~
~~~ ~~~ ~~~ ~~~

~~~ ~~~ ~~~ ~~~
~~~ ~~~ ~~~ ~~~
~~~ ~~~ ~~~
~~~ ~~~ ~~~ ~~~
~~~ ~~~ ~~~ ~~~

Social life
~~~ ~~~ ~~~
~~~ ~~~ ~~~
~~~ ~~~ ~~~
~~~ ~~~ ~~~
~~~ ~~~ ~~~
~~~ ~~~ ~~~
~~~ ~~~ ~~~
~~~ ~~~ ~~~
~~~ ~~~ ~~~ ~~~
~~~ ~~~ ~~~ ~~~
~~~ ~~~ ~~~ ~~~
~~~ ~~~ ~~~ ~~~
~~~ ~~~ ~~~

Show your leaflet or poster to the rest of the class and compare what you have all written. Discuss how easy or difficult it was to write the description.

11 | In business: Business letters

This unit shows you how business letters are normally laid out, presents some useful phrases and gives you practice in writing complete letters.

1 **Business letters are normally laid out in a particular way. Here is an example of one common type of layout called 'block style'.**

```
                                        Haga Nygatan 16C
                                        Göteborg 41709
                                        Sweden

The Manager                             3 January 199#
Muñoz Autos, S.A.
Calle Dia
GRANADA
Spain                                   Your ref: CR67/392

Dear Sir/Madam,

Car Hire 7-14 July 199#

Further to my telephone call today, I am writing to
confirm the details of my reservation.

I would like to book a Sunbeam Camping Van from 7th to
14th July inclusive at the special unlimited mileage rate
of 50,000 pts. a week. I enclose a banker's cheque for
12,500 pts. as a deposit, as requested.

I look forward to hearing from you.

Yours faithfully,

Gunilla Björk (Ms)
```

Note: The letter opens *Dear Sir/Madam* and closes with *Yours faithfully*. Letters which open with a name (e.g. *Dear Mr/Ms/Mrs/Miss Brown*) normally close with *Yours sincerely*.

Look carefully at the letter for a short while and notice where each of the following parts are:

the date	address of sender	name and title of sender
sender's signature	addressee's name and address	message
references		
Dear...	Yours...	a heading

Copy the boxes onto a sheet of paper and then close your books. From memory, see if you can lay them out in 'block style'. Try not to look back!

2 Here are some phrases that are very often used in business letters. What does each phrase *do*? Match each phrase to one of the language functions below. (There are two phrases for function *f*.)

1 *I am writing in connection with* your advertisement in 'The Cyclist' last Thursday.
2 *I am pleased to tell you that* I will be able to attend the interview on Tuesday 26th April.
3 *I would be very grateful if you could* send me your new catalogue as soon as possible.
4 *I am sorry to tell you that* I have to cancel the group holiday which I booked with you.
5 *Thank you for your letter of* 23 July concerning the shoes I purchased from your shop.
6 *Please find enclosed* a cheque for £50 as a deposit.
7 Thank you for the Globe Star radio which arrived today. *Unfortunately,* when I opened the box I found that the power cable was missing.
8 *Unless* you refund my money immediately, *I will be forced to* take legal action.
9 *I must insist that* you return my cheque at once.
10 *I look forward to hearing from you. If you need any further information, I would be very pleased to help you.*
11 Thank you for your invitation to visit your factory. *I would be very pleased to* come on Tuesday 23 September, *if that is convenient for you.*

a) giving good news
b) threatening
c) demanding action
d) requesting action
e) sending something with the letter
f) opening a letter
g) complaining mildly
h) closing a letter
i) giving bad news
j) suggesting

3 Now look at these situations. Write down your opening sentence and main message for each one and then compare with what other people in the class have written.

1 You have seen an advertisement for a job in the newspaper. You want the application forms.
2 You have received a letter from a company which says that you have won a holiday in a competition. It asks you to come to their head office on 15 or 23 March to a prize-giving ceremony.
3 You have received a letter asking you to come for an interview for a job on 16 June. You will be on holiday abroad from 10–24 June.

4 Work in pairs. Choose one of the situations below and write a full letter, laid out in block style. Remember to check your grammar, spelling, phrasing and punctuation, etc. – these things are especially important in business letters.

A

ASLEYS plc	
14 Market Square Buckingham	
ITEM	£ : p
1 pair of gloves	*15-99*
	15-99

You bought a pair of gloves from a shop but when you got home you found that they were both for the left hand. You want to send the gloves back and get a replacement pair.

B

Last night you left your coat in a restaurant in another town. You rang them this morning and they said they would send you the coat if you sent them the money for the postage. You are sending a cheque for £8.00 with your letter, to cover postage.

THE MOUSETRAP RESTAURANT

5 6 Highland Road
Exeter
Devon EX4 7YU
Tel. 675234

C

```
        MAINSTREAM OFFICE SUPPLIES
                5 Kings House
               Leyland LY3 6TH


                          30 March 199#

Dear Madam/Sir,

Order No. 5679/B

Thank you for the recent letter
concerning the above order.

We apologise for the delay in delivering
the fax machine. This is due to problems
at our suppliers. However, we now have
sufficient stocks and will be able to
make delivery within the next 14 days.

With apologies.

Yours faithfully,

Sarah Green

Customer Relations
```

Some time ago you sent £265 for a fax machine. You waited for a month but nothing came so you wrote asking what had happened. In their reply (see the letter), the company said you would get it within two weeks. That was four weeks ago and still nothing has come. You want your money or the fax machine immediately.

When you are ready, give your letter to another pair of students. Write a full reply (laid out in block style) to the letter that you receive:

If you receive a situation A letter, see activity card 2.
If you receive a situation B letter, see activity card 18.
If you receive a situation C letter, see activity card 10.

(Don't look at the other activity cards.)

12 | In business: Journey to paradise?

▶ *IMPORTANT! There are additional teacher's notes on page 85.*

In this unit, you can practise letter writing in a realistic business situation involving two travel companies and a holiday group. You will receive different pieces of information, which you will have to make decisions about, and letters from other groups, which you will have to reply to.

1 **Distant Horizons is a holiday company that offers trips to the Far East and South Pacific. Read their advertisement and find answers to these questions:**
What is *Traveller's World*?
Do the prices of each holiday cover the same things?
If you could go on one of these holidays, which would you choose? Why?

HOLIDAYS IN PARADISE TWO EXCITING NEW TOURS FROM

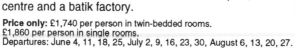
Distant Horizons

Holiday 385B
SUNSHINE IN BALI – 14 nights at the fabulous Sanur Beach, staying in our brand new Excel Hotel. Our special low price includes superb luxury accommodation in a Balinese bungalow right on the beach, half board, all flights, transfers to and from the hotel and excursions to the north of Bali, a kite festival, Balinese temples, a craft centre and a batik factory.

Price only: £1,740 per person in twin-bedded rooms.
£1,860 per person in single rooms.
Departures: June 4, 11, 18, 25, July 2, 9, 16, 23, 30, August 6, 13, 20, 27.

Holiday 386Z **WINTER SPECIAL TO NEW ZEALAND**
14 nights touring the fascinating South Island by luxury coach. Price includes accommodation throughout in the brand new Excel hotels, half board and flights. Your chance to climb glaciers, fly over snow-capped peaks by helicopter and enjoy magnificent skiing in New Zealand.

Price only: £1,535 per person in twin-bedded rooms. £1,660 per person in single rooms.
Departures: June 2, 9, 16, 23, 30, July 6, 13, 20, 27, August 10, 17, 24, 31.

Book now with **Distant Horizons**, 68 Glover St, Bristol, BS6 7HU or with our main agents **Traveller's World**, 67 Lymington Rd, London SW4 6GT.

2 A group of people are trying to book a holiday with Distant Horizons. Unfortunately, things do not go smoothly . . .

In three small groups, you are going to take the parts of Distant Horizons, Traveller's World or the holiday group. The activity cards at the back of the book will give you extra information and tell you who to write to. In your group, you must decide *what* to write, help each other with spellings, grammar, phrasing, etc., and produce full business letters. These should then be delivered to the relevant group (as faxes, where appropriate).

Once you have delivered the letter, ask your teacher for the number of your next activity card. (There are three cards for each group.) The cards will give you some new information for your next letter. You should read all letters that you receive as soon as they arrive – they may affect what you decide to write.

Both Distant Horizons and Traveller's World want the business (Traveller's World also offers holidays with other companies) and the holiday group want to book a holiday, so you will have to work quickly.

If you are Distant Horizons, see activity card 19.
If you are Traveller's World, see activity card 1.
If you are the holiday group, see activity card 9.

3 When the activity is over, look back at the letters that you and the other groups wrote. Can you see any ways to improve the letters? Make a list of the mistakes that you and other students made. You can use the list to check the letters that you write in future.

13 | Advertising: Sell it!

In this unit, you can see how effective advertisements work, look at the vocabulary involved and write some short advertisements yourself.

1 Nowadays, advertising is very big business. Here is some basic advice about designing advertisements. Read through each point and then look at the advertisements on pages 47 and 48. Put a tick in the box if they follow the advice given.

Make your advertisement worth looking at!

Let's face it, most people aren't interested in advertisements – they've got better things to do with their time. So, if you want someone to notice what you want to sell, you have to design your advert carefully. Here are some key points:

1 Put your message in the headline.
If your product is new, then say 'NEW!' If it is improved, then say 'IMPROVED' and *always* put the name of the product in the headline.

2 Say what is special in the headline.
Tell readers what your product offers to them and make it easy to understand.

3 Use positive, emotive words.
You want to give a good impression of your product, so use positive, emotive words like 'high quality', 'unique', 'sophisticated'. Do not use negative words – say what your product *is*, not what it is *not*.

4 Use pictures that say something.
People like pictures. They are easy to 'read'. Use interesting pictures that make readers ask themselves 'What's going on here?'

5 Put a caption beside each picture.
When people see a picture, they look for a caption or a title. Most people do not read the rest of the advertisement. It is a waste of money putting a picture in an advertisement if you are not going to give it a title or caption.

6 Place your company logo clearly in the advertisement.
Your logo will always remind people of what you are trying to sell. Use it on everything!

Advice	1	2	3	4	5	6
Advert A						
B						
C						
D						
E						

A

Spain makes your holiday money go further than any other destination

More beaches to choose from

More for your children

More hotels and restaurants you can afford

More discos to dance the night away

More sights to see

More sun. More fun.

More than ever before, you have to make sure you get real value for money on holiday this year.

Because every holiday resort in Europe has had its fair share of price increases. Including Spain.

The difference is, that in Spain we've made absolutely sure you still get the variety and quality you expect for the pesetas you pay.

Compare what we have to offer to any other destination.

Ask yourself why so many people have already put Spain first this summer. It's simply because our prices still shine through.

ESPAÑA

Spain. Everything under the sun.

Contact your travel agent or the Spanish National Tourist Office, 57 St James's Street, London SW1L 1AD. Telephone 071-499 0901.

B

Enjoy the performance.

The new Scorpio 24 valve. *Ford*

⫸→

C

LEAtHER TRAINERS THAT AREN't MACHINE WASHABLE ST!NK.

K Rapids: guaranteed machine-washable leather for mum, dad and the kids.

K *The shoemakers since 1842.*

D

IN THE GROUNDS OF A REGENCY MANSION

Luxury Self-Catering Holiday Cottages in the heart of the Devonshire countryside. Individually styled and colour co-ordinated, these cottages, forming a courtyard round the old thatched pumphouse, offer elegant and spacious accommodation - set in the beautiful grounds of one of the largest privately-owned country estates in the West Country. Guests have full use of the owner's private club.

Widworthy Court Sports and Leisure Club's facilities include tennis court, squash court, heated outdoor swimming pool, pool-side restaurant, indoor leisure spa complex comprising swimming pool, jacuzzi, sauna, steam room, solarium and bars.

Children and pets welcome
ENJOY THE DIFFERENCE
Please write or telephone for our full colour brochure.
The Manager, The Estate Office, Bridwell Park Estate Uffculme,
Devon EX15 3BU
Telephone (0883) 744783

E

EXPLORE

EXPLORE 1992/93
small group exploratory holidays You'll see more

...in more than 60 countries.

Over 100 exciting tours, treks, safaris and expeditions. Visit ancient sites in Mexico or India, meet the tribals of Morocco, Peru or Thailand, encounter African wildlife, sail a felucca in Egypt, trek in Nepal. Small groups

Our 80-page 1992 colour brochure is packed with superb photos, maps and detailed itineraries -the most original adventure holidays ever organised:

Explore Worldwide (GU),   **Fully Bonded**
1 Frederick Street, Aldershot, Hants   ATOL
GU11 1LQ. ☎ 0252 344161 (24hrs)   2595

When you are ready, see if other students agree with you.

2

Successful advertisements also target the right market. Who would be interested in buying the products below? What positive, emotive words or phrases would you use to describe them? Work with a partner and write down your ideas for each one. For example:

Who might buy it?
people with young children and
money to spare

How can you describe it?
economical
a family car
spacious
reliable
strong, long lasting

'Sunset' – an estate car

'Qualiklen' washing machines

'Henrikson' furniture

'Kraftborr' power tools

'Hansui' audio equipment

'Trojan' bicycles

'Bertolini' fashionable shirts

Some useful words:

smart   efficient   elegant   comfortable   attractive   light   simple
cosy   strong   luxurious   sophisticated   unique   original   tough
powerful   excellent   reliable   soft   quiet

Compare your ideas with other people in your class.

3 Choose one or two of the products in Exercise 2 and, with a partner, write short advertisements. Try to follow the advice in Exercise 1. Look back at the vocabulary in Exercise 2 for ideas. For example:

SUNSET

✳ more colours to choose from
✳ more kilometres to the litre
✳ more space
✳ more comfort
✳ more for your money

The new Sunset 2.5 gives you so much more for your money. It's spacious, reliable and economical.
A pleasure to drive and a pleasure to ride in.

SUNSET. The car for every family.

14 | Advertising: Tastyworld – an advertising campaign

This unit is about 'Tastyworld', a chain of restaurants selling international food. You will work in a small group in order to produce a proposal for an advertising campaign.

TASTYWORLD is a new chain of fast food restaurants with a difference. They sell food from all over the world – but fast. On their menu, they have food from everywhere – Mexican tacos, French snails, Indian curries and lots more – to eat in the restaurant or to take away. The food is fresh and very tasty, at reasonable prices. All types of people go to TASTYWORLD restaurants – young and old people, men and women, business people, students, and families. They aim to make their restaurants fun for everyone.

1 What sort of things do you think TASTYWORLD say in their advertisements?

2 TASTYWORLD have now decided that they need a new advertising campaign because they are planning to open 20 new restaurants. They have asked YOU to help them plan their advertising.

Work in small groups. Each group is an advertising agency, trying to get the contract from TASTYWORLD. TASTYWORLD have asked you to provide some examples of advertisements for them to look at. They would also like a description of where you would place these advertisements, and when. Decide whether you will produce your advertisements and description in the form of a wall display or a file.

Start by thinking about *what* you could advertise. Note down aspects of TASTYWORLD restaurants and details about them (invent anything you like). For example:

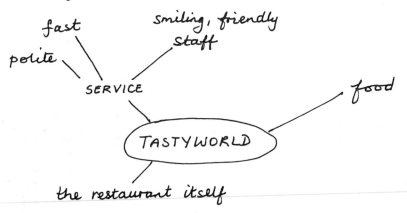

Using these notes, design some short advertisements for TASTYWORLD. For example:

COME INTO A TASTYWORLD
Our smiling, friendly staff will welcome you. Taste the delights of food from all over the world – at prices you can afford . . .

Draw or describe pictures (or use magazine pictures) to show what you would include in your advertisements.

3 When you have finished, show your file or wall display to other groups. When everyone has seen all the proposals, vote to see who would get the TASTYWORLD contract – everybody can have one vote, but you cannot vote for your own proposal.

15 | In the news: Newspaper stories

This unit is about newspaper stories. It focusses on how headlines and photo captions are used, and provides practice in synthesising information for a short newspaper story.

1 Here are some headlines and the first paragraphs of some newspaper stories. Which headline would you put with each story? Compare your answers with your neighbour.
(Notice that newspaper headlines in English are often in the present tense and the main point of the story is usually in the first paragraph.)

£5 'insult' after baby eats glass

Channel ferries lose money

Hoot provokes assault

Gas chief receives second big rise

FIFTY FLEE IN RAIL CRASH FIRE SCARE

A MOTHER whose four-month-old son swallowed 20 slivers of glass from a jar of baby food revealed yesterday she has been sent a £5 voucher as compensation.

Clare Annall, 31, described the gesture by the baby food manufacturer as an insult. Now she is seeking legal advice. She said it was a miracle baby Connor was not seriously injured by the razor-sharp slivers in his mixed fruit puree.

Carole Day, a driving instructor of Camberley, Surrey, beat up Lynne Fairman, a motorist who hooted at her as she was teaching a nervous pupil, Reading Crown Court heard yesterday. She denied assault but was given a conditional discharge and ordered to pay £50 compensation and £500 costs.

A TRAIN was derailed yesterday minutes after rail engineers stopped work and left equipment at the trackside.

Fifty passengers were led to safety from the train.

The last two carriages hit a propane gas cylinder as they left the line. It exploded, starting a fire.

All the passengers on the 7.50am London Victoria to Ramsgate train escaped injury. The driver was among four people treated for shock.

Thousands of commuters fac

THE political row over pay in the boardrooms of privatised companies flared up again yesterday when it was disclosed that Robert Evans, chairman of British Gas, received a 17.6 per cent increase last year, taking his salary to £435,222.

Labour leapt on the increase, reported in the group's annual accounts, to renew its attack on privatisation. Frank Dobson, the energy spokesman, said: "This is another example of the sheer unrivalled greed which has been let loose by setting up privatised monopolies."

STENA, the Swedish shipping group, yesterday blamed losses at its cross channel ferry service, Sealink Stena, for its fall into the red last year.

It did not disclose the extent of the losses on the Sealink Stena business. Overall the Swedish group said it had lost 302 million Swedish crowns (around £30 million), compared with a profit of 225 million Swedish crowns the previous year.

2 Photographs usually have a caption that explains the main point of the story. For example:

Final blow...Richard McKay, of Zero, Mississippi, examines the damage wrought by a tornado which swept through the town before dawn. His foster brother woke the family before the storm, saving their lives.

Look at the photographs. With a partner, decide what the picture is about and then write a suitable short caption. Compare your ideas with other pairs.

You can read the original captions on page 86.

3 Here is a short story about an accident, with an interview script and more details from a news agency. What information from the interview and the agency can you add to the story? Write down the phrases or sentences that you can add and show exactly where you can insert them. (You don't need to add all the extra information.) Then decide on a headline for the story.

A LUNATIC thief almost caused a serious accident when he threw a stolen moped off a bridge at the traffic below.

One driver crashed as she swerved to avoid the Honda 50cc moped. The driver was later treated for shock at Gloucester General Hospital. A police spokesperson said: "It was a crazy thing to do. He could have killed someone."

MOPED ACCIDENT - FURTHER DETAILS:
ACCIDENT HAPPENED NEAR CHANTSWORTH. LORRY DRIVER AND TWO CAR PASSENGERS ALSO HURT. THIEF STOLE MOPED AND BECAME INFURIATED WHEN IT RAN OUT OF PETROL. HE WAS ON THE WAY TO HIS BROTHER'S WEDDING AND WAS ALREADY LATE. ROAD STILL CLOSED. MAN DETAINED BY POLICE.

<u>Interview script</u>
Interviewer: What happened exactly?
Driver: I'm not really sure. I was following the car in front when it suddenly swerved and skidded all over the road.
Interviewer: So what did you do?
Driver: I jammed on my brakes as hard as I could but I ran straight into the back of the car in front. Then the lorry behind hit me.
Interviewer: How fast were you going?
Driver: About ninety kilometres an hour. Like everyone else.
Interviewer: Did you see the moped falling?
Driver: No, but I saw it on the ground. Then a helmet and a jacket came down. There was a man on the bridge shouting and screaming. He was kicking the bridge and swearing at the moped I think.

Compare your ideas with other students in the class.

4

Work with a partner. Look through the information in A, B and C below and make a list of what you think are the main points of news. Like this:

Main points

1. *Unemployment among women is increasing, not men.*
2. *Unemployment among men is ...*
3. *The government says ...*
4. *A local example of the business situation is ...*
5. *...*

News Information

A

UNEMPLOYMENT: JAN–MAR			
	Jan	Feb	Mar
Men	358,321	359,891	356,522
Women	110,010	124,864	143,354
Total	468,331	484,755	499,876
increase		+16,424	+15,121

B

MINISTRY OF EMPLOYMENT
PRESS STATEMENT

This month's unemployment figures show a small increase in unemployment. This is slightly less than the increase last month and brings the total to 499,876. Forecasts, however, indicate that unemployment will begin to fall next month and that this fall will continue until the end of the year. The main increase in this month's figur

C

Local firm announces closure

A LOCAL manufacturer of motor-cycles, Evans Ltd, announced yesterday that it will close at the end of next month.

Evans blames poor sales of its new SupaBike and increases in costs and bank interest rates. The managing director, Eric Evans, said he was sad about the decision but he felt that the company had no other choice. Last year, Evans lost three million pounds and he could see no chance that the situation would improve.

The closure of Evans Ltd will mean the loss of over one thousand jobs in the area, most of them young men and women.

Then, using your list of main points, write a short news article. Begin like this:

UNEMPLOYMENT RISES BY OVER FIFTEEN THOUSAND AGAIN

Unemployment has risen by over fifteen thousand again this month. This brings the total number of unemployed people to ...

When you have finished, sit with another pair. Read through each other's stories and see if you can suggest ways to improve what you have written.

16 | In the news: Newsdesk

▶ *IMPORTANT! There are additional teacher's notes on page 85.*

In this unit, you can simulate the production of the front page of a newspaper. You will need some large sheets of paper, some glue and scissors.

The Citizen, The Daily News, The Daily Standard and **The Post** are large, national newspapers. In small groups, you will work as journalists on the newsdesk of one of these papers. You are trying to produce your front page before the other newspapers.

In your group, you will receive 'news reports' every few minutes. These reports are on the activity cards at the back of the book, but you will not know which stories your group will receive or in which order.

When you receive a report, you must decide what you are going to do with it. You are free to ignore it or make it into a story (you may add any details you want). You will need to work quickly since you are trying to publish your paper before the other newspapers. By the end of the allotted time, you must have your front page ready. Headlines, *the first paragraph* of each story, space for photographs that are coming, captions and so on must all be written and stuck into place.

All groups should start with the news report on activity card 7.

17 | The way we live
Part A: Designing a questionnaire

This unit shows you how to design a questionnaire to investigate the way people live and the different attitudes they have. Unit 18 then shows you how to present the results from your questionnaire.

1 **How do you think most people feel about the way they live? With your neighbour, briefly discuss some of the following questions. Then compare with what other students thought.**

Do most people enjoy their work?   Would they work if they didn't have to?
Is family life still important for most people?
Do young people think very differently about life from older people? If so, how?

2 **Work in small groups. Think of a particular category of people whose lives you are able to discover more about. Then, together, decide on three or four aspects of their lives which you could investigate. Look at the box below for ideas.**

> people 18–25, 25–35, etc.   people working in shops, etc.   men/women at work
> married/single people   with/without children   retired people
>
> home life   family   holidays   leisure   daily routines   health
> money   work   dreams and ambitions   education   social life

Now, for each aspect, make notes about the *facts* and *opinions* you can ask about. For example:

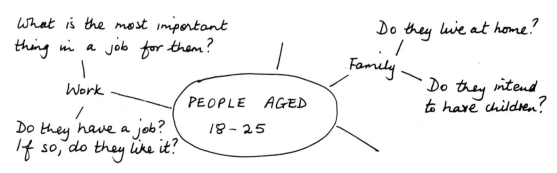

3 When you have finished, show your notes to another group and see if they
can add any points. Then, using your notes, make a questionnaire about
your topics. Decide on five or six questions for each topic and, for each
question, give three or four answers. Like this:

Person

People aged 18-25   1   2   3   etc.

1 Do you work now?
   a) No, and I don't want to.   ☐   ☐   ☐
   b) No, but I'd like to.   ☐   ☐   ☐
   c) Yes, and I enjoy it very much.   ☐   ☐   ☐
   d) Yes, but I hate it.   ☐   ☐   ☐

2 Which is the most important thing in a job for you?
   a) a good salary   ☐   ☐   ☐
   b) lots of free time   ☐   ☐   ☐
   c) interesting work   ☐   ☐   ☐
   d) pleasant people to work with   ☐   ☐   ☐

Exchange questionnaires with another group and read through their
questions. If you have any suggestions to improve their questionnaire, add
some notes. Like this:

Person

People aged 18-25   1   2   3   etc.

1 Do you work now? (- Do you mean 'Do you have a job?')
   a) No, and I don't want to.   ☐   ☐   ☐
   b) No, but I'd like to.   ☐   ☐   ☐
   c) Yes, and I enjoy it very much.   ☐   ☐   ☐
   d) Yes, but I hate it.   ☐   ☐   ☐
      (- You could add an answer: 'Yes, but it's OK.
       I don't like it or dislike it.')

4 Read the comments on your questionnaire and make any changes you feel
necessary. Make sure everyone in the group has a copy of the questionnaire
and then decide exactly how many people you will each try to interview.

Over the next few days, carry out your interviews. (If necessary, translate the
questions for the people you ask.) Have the information you collect ready for
your lesson on Unit 18.

18 | The way we live
Part B: Presenting the results

This unit shows you how to present the results from the questionnaire you designed in Unit 17.

1 With the class, decide how each group will present their findings. For example, you could produce a report or design a poster.

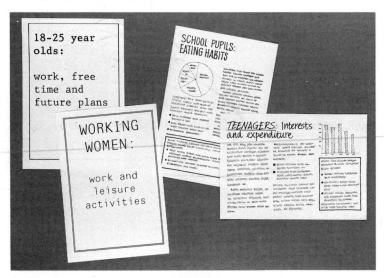

2 In your group, tell each other about the information you collected. Calculate the total number of positive answers to each question. Also note down how many people you interviewed in total.

Which is the most important thing
in a job for you?   ANSWERS   TOTAL = 37
a) a good salary   8
b) lots of free time   17
c) interesting work   6
d) pleasant people to work with   6

3   Now, in your group, decide what you can say about the results of the questionnaire. Together, write a summary of your findings. (Alternatively, divide the information between you so that each person can write about a different part of the questionnaire. Together, read through what each person writes and make changes so that it forms a complete summary.)

We interviewed a total of 37 people aged between 18 and 25 about their attitudes to work, the way they spend their free time and their plans for the future. In connection with their attitudes to work, about half of the people said that the most important thing for them in a job was to have a lot of free time. Less than a quarter thought that a good salary, interesting work or pleasant people to work with were the most important things. We also asked them if they liked their job at the moment. Most people said they enjoyed it although nearly a quarter said that they hated their work.
    In connection with their free time, we asked them if ...

Some useful expressions:

a quarter/half/three quarters   fifty/sixty/etc. per cent   with regard to . . . ,
in comparison with . . .   concerning . . . ,   in connection with . . . ,

4   You can also present your findings in visual form, as a bar or pie chart.

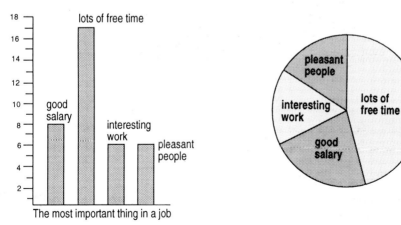

5   When you have finished, read through each other's reports or posters. What things do the people you interviewed have in common? In what ways are they different?

19 | A class newspaper
Part A: Planning the paper

*This unit and Unit 20 help you to start a class newspaper and produce your
first issue. In this unit, you decide what will be in your newspaper and write
an opinion column. In Unit 20, you write the articles and features for your
paper and assemble your first issue.*

1   Work as a class. Here are some ideas for sections of a class newspaper. Read
through each one and discuss what you could write about. What other
sections could you have? Add them to the plan.

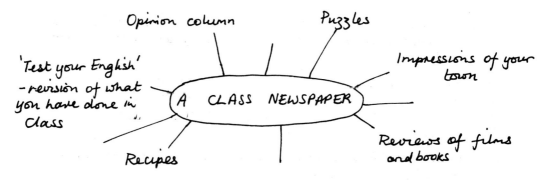

2   You will need to make some basic decisions. Discuss these questions about
how you will produce the paper:

Will you be able to photocopy it or will it be displayed as a poster on the
    wall?
What size paper will you use?
Do you want to give the paper a name?
Where can you get pictures to include in the paper?
When do you want to have your first issue ready?

3 You will need to decide how much space to allow for articles. On a piece of paper the same size as your newspaper, design a basic layout with different sized spaces. Like this:

Keep this basic plan to hand or put it on the wall.

4 For the first issue, write a class opinion column where each person says what he or she thinks about a topic. Choose a subject that you will all write about. For example:

The best and worst things about . . .   being a man/woman   studying
working as a . . .   living in (country)   food from (country)
owning a (car, animal, etc.)   Three things I really can't stand: . . .
What I would do if . . .   A day on my own

By yourself, write down your opinion on the topic your class chose. Give a reason for each point you mention.

For me, the best thing about being a student is the amount of free time I have. I only have 12 hours of lectures a week so I can do things when I feel like doing them.

Compare your ideas with a neighbour. Help each other with spelling, grammar, phrasing, and so on.

5 Look at your plan from Exercise 3 and decide how much space you want for the class opinion column. Then, on one piece of paper the same size as the space, each person should write their ideas from Exercise 4. Pass the paper around the class while you are working on Unit 20.

20 | A class newspaper
Part B: The first issue

This unit shows how the ideas presented in Unit 19 can be developed into sections for the first issue of your newspaper. You will need some large sheets of paper, glue and scissors.

1 **Look at the ideas you discussed in Unit 19, Exercise 1. Choose a section that you would like to write. Below are instructions to help with some of the sections but you can choose any section you prefer. You can do this by yourself, in pairs or in a small group.**

While you are writing, ask the other students and your teacher for ideas or for help with spelling, grammar, phrasing, and so on.

A PUZZLES

Make a crossword puzzle for the paper. Like this:

- First draw a square 10 × 10. Divide it into smaller squares and then write in some words across and down. Put ■ in the squares you do not need. (You can also write in abbreviations.)
- Number the start of each word.
- Write a clue for each word. For example, for 'water' this could be a definition (e.g. *A liquid made of hydrogen and oxygen*), a sentence with a missing word (e.g. *Seventy-five per cent of the Earth's surface is _____*), or a cryptic clue (e.g. *The gap between the English and the Americans*). Give each clue the same number as the word. Divide the clues into two groups: clues for words that go *across* and clues for words that go *down*.

	¹T	²H	³I	⁴N		⁵O	N	L	Y
		⁶W	I	N	T	E	R		
⁷T	O						⁸O	N	⁹E
			¹⁰W	¹¹A	T	¹²E	R		¹³A	A
¹⁴C	¹⁵A	R	T		M		¹⁶E	R	R
	¹⁷P	I	E		P				
¹⁸G	E	T		¹⁹S	T	E	A	²⁰M	
U		E		²¹E	Y			²²O	²³E
L					A			²⁴T	O	N
²⁵P	U	Z	Z	L	E		²⁶A	N	D

64

– When you have written all the clues check that they are in correct English and that the clue numbers match the numbers shown in the crossword.

Now choose a space on the plan you made in Unit 19, Exercise 3 and sign your name(s) on it. On a piece of paper the same size as the space, copy the square (without the words!). Write the clues underneath.

B   TEST YOUR ENGLISH

Look back through your coursebook and write an exercise to test something you have learnt recently. It could, for example, be a scrambled matching exercise:

nanaba   the opposite of wide

rornaw   ⌐ something to eat with

hiktsoccp ⌐   a type of fruit

or a scrambled dialogue that you have written:

– we I'm sorry, have that don't size any .
– you Thank .
– I'd new this battery camera, like please for a .
– of Yes course . the next the chemist corner Try on .
– I could tell Oh me dear, where get can one you ?

When you have written and checked your exercise, choose a space on the layout plan and sign your name(s) on it. Copy the exercise onto a piece of paper the same size as the space.

C   IMPRESSIONS OF YOUR TOWN

Think for a few minutes about your impressions of the town where you live and the people who live there. (If you are working in a small group, some of you could think about the town and the others could think about the people.) Note down your ideas.

The people

a lot of young people
many people live in houseboats
accommodation shortage
squatters

The town

large, noisy city
always very busy
very beautiful in the old part
the canals

⟫⟫→

Now, using your ideas, write about your impressions of the town.

Amsterdam : a personal impression

Amsterdam is a large, noisy city. It's always very busy and, at any time of the day or night, you can find people out on the streets. The best part of the city is the old part. Here, you can find beautiful old buildings along the edge of the canals, many of which date back to 1600 or earlier. This part of Amsterdam has a very special atmosphere for me. Walking through its narrow streets in the early hours of the morning, you can imagine how it was long ago. ...

Amsterdam attracts a lot of young people and, as a result, there is a very severe shortage of accommodation. In the past, this has led to 'squatters' taking over some of the empty buildings. Other people have chosen to make their home on the water in one of the hundreds of houseboats along the edge of the canals...

When you have written about your impressions and checked your work, choose a space on the layout plan and sign your name(s) on it. Copy out your paragraphs onto a piece of paper the same size as the space.

D   RECIPES

Do you know any unusual or typical recipes? Make a list of the ingredients that you need and write step-by-step instructions. Say where the recipe is from and when it is normally eaten.

Buñuelos

This is a sweet eaten in Mexico, especially around Christmas time.

Ingredients

1 kg plain flour
3 eggs
1 teaspoon baking powder
1 tablespoon vegetable fat
water
cooking oil
2 cups of sugar and star anise or honey

Delicious!

1 Mix the flour, eggs, baking powder and fat with some water to make a ball.
2 Knead this ball until small bubbles appear and it does not stick to the board.
3 Cover it and leave it to stand for one hour.
4 Make little balls the size of golf balls from the mixture and roll them out very thinly.
5 Deep fry them in hot oil, drain and leave them to cool.
6 Serve them with a syrup made with the sugar, water and star anise or warm honey.

When you are able to see how much space you need, choose a place on the layout plan and sign your name(s) on it. Copy out your recipe onto a piece of paper the same size as the space.

E   REVIEWS OF FILMS AND BOOKS

Choose a film or a book that you have seen or read recently. First note down the *facts* about the story and then your *opinion* of it. Using your notes, write your review. You could award it stars (one to five) to show what you think.

"Ragtime" by E.L. Doctrow is a complex book, mixing fact with fiction to portray life in New York at the turn of the century. The main plot concerns a negro pianist, Mr Walker, who, after suffering racist attacks by the city firemen, attempts to extract a public apology from the fire chief. When all the official channels have been tried without success, Walker then decides to take things into his own hands. With a group of collaborators, he takes over a library building and ...

"Ragtime" is a very enjoyable book to read and it shows Doctrow's considerable skill as a novelist. Numerous famous characters, including Houdini, the illusionist, and Booker T. Washington, the negro educationist, enter into the book, helping to make the story a very convincing one. I found the book extremely interesting and ...

* * * * *

When you have finished, choose a place on the layout plan and sign your name(s) on it. Copy out your review onto a piece of paper the same size as the space.

If you finish before everyone else in the class, see if you can write something more for the paper. Look at the ideas in Unit 19, Exercise 1 and choose a topic.

2   **When everyone is ready, stick each section onto your layout, moving articles and pictures around to fill the space. Photocopy your newspaper or put it up as a poster. You could give a copy to another class (perhaps in another school) and ask if they can also produce a paper for you.**

⋙→

3 For future issues, you can work on some of the other ideas you discussed in Unit 19, Exercise 1. You could also choose a new topic for the opinion column and get everyone to write their views.

Before you start a new issue, look back at the questions in Unit 19, Exercise 2. Are there any things you need to or would like to change for your next issue? Is it possible for you to get the paper typed next time? Do you need an editor to put the next issue together?

Activity cards

Card 1

You have just heard from contacts in Bali that work has not yet started on the Excel Hotel at Sanur Beach. All Distant Horizons holidays to Bali are going to use this hotel. You do not want to take bookings on holidays that might not be able to go ahead. You have telephoned Distant Horizons but you cannot get a clear answer. Write and ask them what is happening.

Letter plan
– *Dear . . .*
– put a heading
– tell them what you have heard
– ask them to explain the situation
– close the letter (*We look forward to . . .*)
– sign it
When you have delivered your letter to Distant Horizons, ask for a new card number.

Card 2

You are the manager of Asleys plc. You are very sorry about the problem with the gloves. You will send a new pair of gloves in a separate packet and a pair of your fashion socks as a gift. Write to the person who sent you the letter to tell him or her this.

Card 3

STORMS AT SEA: ONE SHIP LOST
A ship was lost from radio contact last night. It is not known what has happened. Planes and helicopters are now searching the area.
Details:
    Name of ship: Sea Queen
    Carrying: wood
    Crew: 15, Swedish captain
    Sailing from Sweden to Spain

Card 4

NEW TAXES AND TAX RATES ANNOUNCED THIS MORNING
Tax on petrol increased from 50% to 75%
Tax on cigarettes increased from 50% to 75%
Tax on luxury goods (radios, TVs, cars, etc.) increased from 20% to 28%
Tax on basic goods (food, clothes, books, etc.) increased from 10% to 15%
NEW TAX: 10% tax on all telephone calls
NEW TAX: 12% tax on all air tickets
NEW TAX: airport tax of US$10 for each international departure

Card 5

You have just heard that the new Excel Hotels in New Zealand and Bali
(which your company intends to use) will not be ready in time for next June.
Because of this, you cannot accept any bookings for Holidays 385B and
386Z. Write to your main agent and to anyone from whom you have
received a booking.

Letter plan
– Dear . . .
– put a heading
– give the bad news and explain why you cannot accept any bookings
– close the letter
– sign it
When you have delivered the letters, ask for a new card number.

Card 6

PERSON A
Name: Alex Thoms
Home: A small flat in a tall block of flats in the suburbs of a city
Place of work: A bank
Interests: Sports, pictures, music, dance, food, racing
Family: Married with three children

Card 7

PROBLEMS WITH THE ECONOMY: PM WILL NOT RESIGN
Text of interview with TV reporter Jane Kinley

JK: Prime Minister, in recent months there have been a number of calls for you to resign because of the state of the economy. How do you respond to those calls?

PM: It is my view that the economy is in a very strong position. I accept that there have been some difficulties in recent months but we believe that the economy is basically very strong. We expect to see the situation improving within the next three to four months.

JK: So you do not accept a call for you to resign?

PM: I do not.

JK: In what situation would you resign?

PM: I cannot answer that question.

JK: Prime Minister, would you agree that the government's economic policy has been a failure? We have very high levels of unemployment, inflation is increasing and now we may have a strike of railway workers.

PM: I have said that I believe that the economy is strong. These are difficult times but we can see light at the end of the tunnel.

JK: What, if anything, will the government do about the latest increases in inflation?

PM: We will announce some new steps to reduce inflation towards the end of this week.

JK: What will those steps be?

PM: I am afraid I cannot give further details at the moment.

JK: Will the government increase taxes?

PM: The government has said on numerous occasions that it does not see any need to increase taxes.

Photograph coming of PM outside government building.

Card 8

You were going to move to a new town but you have now decided not to. Write and thank the person for the leaflets anyway.

Card 9

In your group, decide:
- which of the two holidays you want to go on together
- how many single or twin-bedded rooms you will need
- when you want to go (check the dates in the advertisement)
  and then write a letter to Distant Horizons to book the holiday
  (your address is: 151 New Road, Birmingham BR8 4TW).

Letter plan
- open the letter (*Dear . . ., We are writing . . .*)
- say what you want to book (*We would like to book . . .*)
- close the letter (*We look forward to . . .*)
- sign it (choose a group leader)

When you have delivered your letter to Distant Horizons, ask for a new card number.

Card 10

You work in the Customer Relations department at Mainstream Office Supplies. You are sorry about the delays. Unfortunately, the AZ6300 fax machine is not available any more. Instead, you will receive a new model, the AZ6400, which is a much better machine. You hope to deliver it when it becomes available soon. Write to the person who wrote to you and tell him or her this.

Card 11

POP STAR GIVES $2 MILLION TO CHARITY
Pop star Ricardo Sanchez (27, born Mexico City) last night announced his intention to give $2 million to the International Children's Aid organisation. ICA works mainly in Latin America. Photographs of Sanchez coming.

Card 12

UNEMPLOYMENT FIGURES: MAY TO AUGUST

	May	June	July	Aug
Men	556,987	573,132	598,556	652,765
increase		+16,145	+25,424	+54,209
Women	364,543	373,111	385,786	434,175
increase		+8,568	+12,675	+48,389
Total	921,530	946,243	984,342	1,086,940
increase		+24,713	+38,099	+102,598

Card 13

You eventually managed to speak to Traveller's World. They said they could arrange the same holiday as the one with Distant Horizons but much more cheaply with another company called Compass Tours. You have therefore made a reservation with them. Write two short letters.

1 A letter to Distant Horizons to cancel your booking with them:

Letter plan
  – *Dear . . .*
  – put a heading
  – say what you are writing about (. . . *our booking for X people on the holiday to . . .*)
  – give the bad news
  – close the letter
  – sign it

2 A letter to Traveller's World to confirm your reservation:

Letter plan
  – *Dear . . .*
  – put a heading
  – say what you are writing about (. . . *our telephone conversation about . . .*)
  – confirm your reservation with Compass Tours (*We would like to confirm . . . for X people on a tour to . . .*)
  – close the letter
  – sign it

Card 14

Unfortunately, you will be away when the person comes to Australia. Write and tell him or her.

Card 15

INFLATION RATES: JANUARY TO SEPTEMBER

Annual inflation rates

Jan	Feb	Mar	Apr	May
15.6%	19.7%	23.6%	25.0%	30.0%

June	July	August	Sept	
25.6%	28.7%	29.9%	32.7%	

Prediction for October: 35.7%

Card 16

TRAIN CRASH: FURTHER DETAILS
All people injured have now been released from hospital. Firemen
took over 8 hours to free an elderly lady from the wreckage. National
Rail company will begin an investigation tomorrow. Trains were 25
years old.

Card 17

FURTHER STORMS EXPECTED
Weather experts today predicted further strong winds of over
160kph and heavy rain for two to three days more. They advise
people to stay at home.
Detailed weather chart coming.

Card 18

You are the manager of The Mousetrap Restaurant. You did have the coat
but now you cannot find it. You think that somebody took it by mistake.
Write to the person who wrote to you and offer him or her a free meal at
your restaurant as compensation. Return their cheque.

Card 19

The airline which your company uses has increased its charges by 5%
because of an increase in oil prices. This means that the prices of your
holidays will also have to rise (New Zealand £1,565 twin, £1,690 single; Bali
£1,770 twin, £1,890 single). Write to Traveller's World (your main agent)
and inform them of this.

Letter plan
– *Dear . . .*
– put a heading
– give the bad news and explain why your prices have risen (*This is because
  of . . .*)
– close the letter
– sign it

When you have delivered your letter to Traveller's World, ask for a new card
number.

Card 20

PERSON B
Name: Daniel Carrillo
Home: A large flat in the suburbs of a city
Place of work: A bank
Interests: Sports, pictures, music, dance, food, racing
Family: Married with three children

Card 21

STORMS CAUSE EXTENSIVE DAMAGE: FURTHER DETAILS
A school roof in the north of the country was completely ripped off
by winds. No injuries.
Falling trees have closed a further 25 main roads.
Coastal towns have been flooded.
The river in the capital has burst its banks. The city centre is closed to
all traffic.
Photograph coming of school building.

Card 22

The socks are definitely yours but you don't know anything about the shoe.
You have found the jumper. It was in the back of your car.

Card 23

PM OFFERS RESIGNATION TO PRESIDENT
Text of a letter sent this afternoon:

FROM THE OFFICE OF THE PRIME MINISTER

Mr President,

As you know, during the last few months, my health has not been good.
Despite the fact that I have had two successful operations, my left leg
continues to give me great pain. As you will appreciate, this has made
it very difficult for me to carry out my work as Prime Minister with
the attention which it deserves. I have tried, over the last few
months, to find ways in which I could continue but I am sorry to say
that I feel this is no longer possible. It is, therefore, with deep
regret that I write now to offer my resignation with effect from today.

Yours,

G.T. WENSLO

Card 24

You have just seen this advertisement in the newspaper.

Traveller's World TRAVEL AGENTS
Special Offers

14 day half board all inclusive holidays in first class hotels (+ single
supplement) from:

Mexico (Oaxaca, Cancun, Merida)	£1347 (+50)
Thailand (Chang Mai, Bangkok, Koh Samui)	£1335 (+45)
United States (New York, Chicago, San Francisco, Los Angeles)	£980 (+55)

also special low prices to Bali, New Zealand, Australia and Tahiti

TRAVELLER'S WORLD, 67 Lymington Rd, London SW4 6GT
Tel 081 786 1897, Fax 081 786 4444

You have tried ringing Traveller's World but they are always engaged. Write
a letter to them and ask if they can arrange the same holiday that you chose
with Distant Horizons (give the dates and details of the holiday). Ask how
much it would cost.

When you have delivered your letter to Traveller's World, ask for a new card
number.

Card 25

Text of radio interview with pop star Ricardo Sanchez
(Interviewer Kerstin Ohara)

KO: You have recently announced that you will give a large sum of money
   to ICA. How much do you intend to give?

RS: I have already given about five hundred thousand dollars and I intend
   to give another five hundred thousand.

KO: There were earlier reports that you intended to give two million.

RS: I don't know where those reports came from. I'm giving a total of one
   million dollars.

KO: You have said that you want to help the International Children's Aid
   organisation. Why are you particularly interested in ICA?

RS: ICA have done a tremendous amount of work in my home country of
   Mexico and I just want to say thank you to them. They have helped
   thousands of children throughout Latin America.

Card 26

You received a telephone booking for a group holiday. Write to the people confirming that there is space available on all Compass Tours holidays and confirming your prices: New Zealand (South Island tour) £1,445 twin, £1,515 single; Bali (Sanur Beach + excursions) £1,600 twin, £1,670 single. Their address is: 151 New Road, Birmingham BR8 4TW.

Letter plan
- put a heading
- say why you are writing (*We are writing to confirm . . .*)
- give the details
- close the letter (*We look forward to . . .*)
- sign it

Card 27

You think it is a wonderful idea. Write and say that you would love to go.

Card 28

PERSON C
Name: Ben Lucas
Home: A large house with a large garden in the suburbs of a city
Place of work: A bank
Interests: Sports, pictures, music, dance, food, racing
Family: Married with three children

Card 29

Your head office has made a new agreement with the Sunwood hotels in New Zealand and Bali. This means that you are now able to accept bookings on holidays 385B and 386Z. Unfortunately, the prices will have to rise by a total of 10%, including the oil price increase (New Zealand £1,688 twin, £1,826 single; Bali £1,914 twin, £2,046 single). Write to Traveller's World and anybody who has a booking with you.

Letter plan
- *Dear . . .*
- give the good news
- give the bad news (*Unfortunately, . . .*)
- close the letter (*We look forward to . . .*)
- sign it

Card 30

DETAILS OF INTERNATIONAL CHILDREN'S AID
ORGANISATION
Headquarters: Toronto, Canada
Established: 1986
Annual income: $5.6 million
Projects: Mexico: 5 children's hospitals, 10 rural schools, flying
doctor service, 3 orphanages; Nicaragua: 2 children's hospitals and 2
orphanages; Colombia: 1 children's hospital, flying doctor service

Card 31

TRAIN CRASH
At 16.30pm, 45 people injured, 0 seriously. Two trains hit head on at
central station. Driver says brakes failed. Central station now closed.
All trains will leave from northern station instead. 3–6 hour delays
on all trains to the north and west. Photograph coming.

Card 32

STORMS CAUSE EXTENSIVE DAMAGE
Winds of over 160kph caused extensive damage last night. Police
report 189 roads blocked. All trains and boats cancelled.

Card 33

Your head office has recently made an agreement with another company,
called Compass Tours, to offer holidays to Mexico, New Zealand, Thailand,
USA and Bali all at lower prices than Distant Horizons. You have therefore
decided to cancel your agreement with Distant Horizons. Write and tell them
this.

Letter plan
– *Dear . . .*
– put a heading
– tell them about your new agreement
– give the bad news
– close the letter
– sign it

When you have delivered your letter to Distant Horizons, ask for a new card
number.

About *Writing 3*

Writing 3 is the third of four writing books in the *Cambridge Skills for Fluency* series. As the approach taken to writing in this and the other three books in the series may be unfamiliar to some teachers and students, the notes which follow outline the basic principles behind the materials and offer some general guidance for their use. These notes are set out under five main questions: Who is *Writing 3* for?; What is the purpose of the book?; How is the book organised?; What kind of activities does the book provide?; and How should the book be used?

1 Who is *Writing 3* for?

Writing 3 is intended for students with an upper-intermediate knowledge of English who may be studying in language institutes or in the upper classes of secondary schools.

2 What is the purpose of the book?

Writing 3 has two basic aims: firstly, to develop the skill of writing itself; and, secondly, to develop general language proficiency through writing. The second of these aims may seem unusual in 'skills' materials, so some explanation follows.

Writing, as a means of developing students' general abilities in English, is greatly undervalued in most language courses. Apart from the occasional letter-writing or descriptive paragraph task, general language courses usually restrict writing to tasks such as filling gaps or writing isolated sentences as part of a grammar exercise. Yet there are a number of good reasons for bringing writing into a more central position in classroom work.

Firstly, in contrast to oral classroom work, writing can offer students the opportunity to work at their own pace and, above all, to think while they are producing language. Many students feel very anxious when they are called upon to speak in front of others and this anxiety effectively blocks their ability to think clearly. Handled correctly, writing can be less stressful. Secondly, writing can give students a chance to retrace their steps, to check and correct what they have written before they are required to show it to another person. This can allow more room for students to develop confidence in their language abilities, to develop their own understanding of how the language works and of what is 'linguistically possible'. Thirdly, unlike oral classroom work, writing can offer a permanent record; students can look back on what they have done, improve, check things, and refresh their memory of what they learnt in class. For these reasons, writing can offer students considerable opportunities to increase their vocabulary, to refine their knowledge of the grammar, and to develop their understanding of how things are best expressed and how well their message is understood. In short, writing can offer more opportunities to learn.

In addition to the potential role of writing in general language development, however, there is also a 'skill' element to be considered – those abilities which are specific to writing itself. There are at least four main aspects to this. Firstly, there is knowledge of the different *types* of writing and the conventions of each (e.g. letters, postcards, messages, notices, reports, poems, etc.). Secondly, there is an understanding of the *function* of a piece of writing and how that is accomplished. Is it intended to amuse? To inform? To persuade? and so on. Thirdly, there is an understanding of the *structure* of a piece of writing. How is the text put together? Is there an introduction? How are examples given? How does the text end? and so on. Finally, there is the matter of the *process* of writing itself. What steps does the writer go through to produce a text? There are probably as many different ways of approaching writing as there are writers, but some common ways one can identify are 'brainstorming' (jotting down points as they occur to you), making and organising notes, writing drafts, revising, writing spontaneously, dictating aloud to oneself, and so on. As far as is relevant for students of General English at this level, the Writing books aim to develop each of these four aspects of writing. Through the Writing books as a whole, students are presented with many types of written text, are asked to consider their purpose and structure and are also introduced to numerous ways in which they can approach their own writing (see question 4 below).

3   How is the book organised?

The book contains 20 units built around different topics. Each of these units is intended to cover approximately 50–60 minutes of classroom work, although this will vary considerably, depending on the abilities of the students and the pace at which they work. (The 'extension' tasks in Units 1–8 are intended for use if you have more time available.) A number of the units are in pairs (see, for example, Units 9 and 10, 11 and 12). These develop a topic over two units, although each unit is entirely free-standing and may be done individually, without the need to do the other unit in the pair. The exceptions to this are Units 17 and 18, 19 and 20 where students will need to have done Part A before proceeding to Part B.

Generally, the activities at the beginning of a unit concentrate on work at the level of vocabulary or planning out ideas, whilst those towards the end of the unit demand more extended writing. In the case of the paired units, the first unit normally consists of a series of introductory tasks familiarising students with various aspects of writing such as synthesising news items to form a news report or the language and conventions of letter writing. The second unit then draws on these abilities in the context of a 'whole task' such as the production of the front page of a newspaper or the exchange of business correspondence to secure a holiday booking. Typically, students work in groups during these activities, often referring to cards at the back of the book which supply additional information during the course of their writing.

4 What kind of activities does the book provide?

As was mentioned above, the first purpose of the book, the development of writing skills, is accomplished by introducing various types of written texts (e.g. letters, reports, summaries, poems, newspaper articles, captions and so on), by asking students to consider the purpose of elements of a text, by identifying the structure of a text, and by encouraging students to try out different ways in which to approach their own writing. Most of these aspects, however, are not explicitly set out in the materials themselves, although the *Map* at the beginning of the book should enable you to locate a particular aspect of writing should you wish to do so. The aim has been to integrate the various aspects of writing as naturally as possible into the development of a particular topic so that students experience them as 'ways of working' rather than 'things to be learnt'.

In *Writing 3*, particular effort has been taken to develop the range of strategies which students may use in the process of writing. These are offered not as prescriptions but as opportunities to experience and experiment with different ways of going about writing. The students themselves may then make their own decisions about what works best for them as individuals. Below is a list of some of the strategies which are introduced in the book, together with references to example exercises.

– making 'idea maps' (e.g. 14.2)
– using questions to plan writing (e.g. 1.3, 3.2)
– making notes before writing (e.g. 1.2, 2.3)
– incorporating reader reactions (e.g. 3.3, 9.3)
– comparing/sharing ideas with others before writing (e.g. 7.1, 19.1)
– comparing/sharing ideas with others whilst writing (e.g. 1.3, 6.2, 10.3)
– comparing/sharing reactions after writing (e.g. 3.5, 6.4)
– drawing various sources of information together (e.g. 15.3)
– devising correction checklists (e.g. 7.5, 12.3)
– designing own practice exercises (e.g. 4.2)
– keeping a learning diary (e.g. 4.4)
– logical thought techniques (e.g. 8.1–8.5)

In fulfilling the second purpose of the writing books, general language development, *Writing 3* aims to provide open-ended, creative, imaginative tasks which will stimulate students to use language to say what they wish to say and improve their fluency. You will find, therefore, few exercises with clearly right or wrong answers and few which require students to simply copy or produce 'parallel' texts. Many of the activities are interactive – that is, they require students to write to, for and with other students. The aim in doing this is to encourage students to talk about writing and, thereby, learn from each other. Through working in groups to produce a piece of writing, students have an opportunity to ask each other – and the teacher if need be – about spelling, vocabulary, grammar, and the best ways of expressing things. Interactive writing tasks also give students a unique opportunity to get feedback from their readers on how far their message has been understood and, in so doing, fully integrate writing with the other three main skills – listening, speaking and reading.

5   How should the book be used?

If you are using the book to support your other classroom work, the *Map* at the beginning of the book will help you select a particular unit. The *Map* details the topic and main aspects of writing involved in each unit. The instructions for each of the tasks in the book are addressed directly to students, thereby making it easier for both teachers and students to see what is expected. It is hoped that these instructions are clear enough to make further, detailed guidance for the teacher unnecessary but some general notes on the use of the materials may, however, be useful.

In developing the students' abilities to write in English, one of the most important principles is that they are given time to think, write, revise and discuss with their neighbours and are not unduly rushed. With a class that contains students of varying levels of ability, this may mean that you find that some students finish before others. A useful technique to reduce this problem is to 'chunk' tasks, that is, to ask students to do two or three tasks before they return to whole class discussion. In this way, once students have finished a task, they can move straight on to a further task without waiting for others.

While students are writing, the teacher's job will mainly consist of circulating around the room. The key is for the teacher to be available and not to make students feel defensive of their writing. Writing is unfortunately very commonly used as a means of evaluation so it is not surprising that many people feel they are being judged when someone reads what they have written. If students do have problems in writing, some teachers find it productive to give hints or clues to students rather than direct answers, since this helps students to develop the ability to write without assistance. It is worthwhile, for instance, keeping a few bilingual (and English–English) dictionaries and grammars available so that students can check things for themselves without having to ask the teacher all the time. Although this may appear slow and time-wasting, it will help students develop habits which they will almost certainly need when the course is over.

It is often quite useful to provide background music while students are working. This could be classical music, jazz, blues – anything, although it is important to choose something that will not put anyone off. The mood of the music is also significant – if the writing activity involves two stages, one of a group/pair writing and the other of comparison with other groups/pairs, you might choose some calm, relaxing music for the first stage but something more energetic for the second stage.

Many of the activities in the book involve students working in pairs or small groups of three or possibly four students (three is usually the best number as it allows more opportunities for students to contribute their ideas). It is usually best to let the students know how much time they have for group work, so that they know when they have to present their ideas or writing to the class. At the upper-intermediate level for which *Writing 3* is intended, one may expect group discussions to be taking place in English, although it is important to recognise that use of the mother tongue may be necessary for students in order to clarify their understanding and exchange ideas. An 'English only' rule may thus be counter-productive in these situations, making communication difficult and defeating one of the purposes of group work – to encourage students to help each other and share ideas. The most important thing is that what finally emerges from group work is a piece of written English.

In setting up group work, it is usually advisable to suggest that *all* the students within the group write, building up their own copy of the text which the group is collaboratively producing. This will ensure that all the students involved gain maximum benefit from the group work, focussing on both the meaning and form of what is being written. Students involved in such group work typically get involved in asking each other about spellings, re-reading what they have already written and in suggesting changes to grammar, phrasing and so on. Despite its obvious benefits, however, collaborative writing is not without its problems. For many students, the collaborative tasks in *Writing 3* will be the first time they have ever produced a piece of written work *with* someone else. For this reason, you may find it useful to devote some time after a group writing task to discuss how the activity went, what problems the students had in their groups and how they may improve their group work next time.

Once the students have written a complete text and they have had an opportunity to discuss and compare ideas, it may be useful to spend some time looking at the *form* of what they have written – that is, the grammar, punctuation, spelling, phrasing and so on. In practice, many of the difficulties which students encounter in writing are often resolved through discussion while they are writing (for example, it is my experience that students frequently correct and revise their own work after having had the opportunity to read and compare with another student's work). Nevertheless, teachers and students may feel it necessary or useful to focus specifically on the accuracy of their writing. This could be done in a variety of ways. Students could, for example, be given some time to look back over their work (in pairs or individually) and to identify any things they are not sure of and which they would like to ask other students or the teacher about. During this time, the teacher could circulate around the class, reading through the students' work. A supply of dictionaries and grammars would, once again, be useful during this time.

Alternatively, some teachers may prefer to collect in written work for correction. One useful idea for this is to adopt a marking scheme. This involves putting a symbol in the margin indicating the kind of mistake that has been made (e.g. sp = spelling, w/w = wrong word, T = tense, w/m = word missing, w/o = word order is wrong, w/f = wrong form, e.g. 'It were good', ? = I don't understand!). This means that students then have to discover for themselves what is wrong, and thus develop the ability to work independently of the teacher.

Writing 3 aims to provide a range of interesting and useful material which will enrich your language course. The tasks aim to develop the students' abilities to write in English, and to give them an opportunity to use English to say what they wish to say. We hope that you enjoy using it.

Teacher's notes for Units 12 and 16

Unit 12

This activity simulates a business situation in which two companies compete for business from a holiday group. The activity can be done in one 50-minute lesson if the students write fairly quickly, or in two 50-minute lessons with more time for discussion and feedback. If you are short of time, the students can prepare their first letter before the lesson. The lesson can then begin with them discussing their already completed letters before delivering one of them to the appropriate group.

If you have more than 12 students, you can form two or more sets of three groups. Before you start the activity, ensure that the students understand the basic situation and what is expected of them. *All* the students within each group should write, to gain maximum benefit from the activity. There are three activity cards for each group. Once a group has delivered a letter to the appropriate group, you can then tell them their next role card number (i.e. they do not have to wait for other groups to finish). However, the groups will need to be more or less at the same stage in the activity.

On page 87, there are letterheads for the two companies which you can photocopy onto blank sheets of paper for students to use when writing their letters.

The role card numbers are as follows:
Distant Horizons: 19 then 5 then 29
Traveller's World: 1 then 33 then 26
Holiday group: 9 then 24 then 13

Unit 16

You will need some large sheets of paper (for example, A3), glue and scissors for each group. On page 88 you will find newspaper mastheads which you may like to photocopy for use in the activity.

The activity can be done in one or two 50-minute lessons, depending on the number of news stories you refer the students to and how quickly you feel that they work. You will need to allow 10 minutes for students to see each other's newspapers at the end. If you would like to save time, ask the students to read card 7 before the lesson. (This activity works most successfully with three to four students in each group.)

On a piece of paper, copy, in a *random order*, the activity card numbers below and then cross out any five numbers. Make a different random list for each group. These lists show the order in which you will give the students the news reports. Important: the students must not see your lists of card numbers!

As students receive news reports, they are to write the first paragraph of the story, decide on a headline and, if they intend to use one of the photographs which are 'coming', write a caption. They should write their paragraphs, headlines and captions on separate pieces of paper which they can then move around and glue into place on the large sheet to form the front page.

Before you start the activity, tell the students how much time they have. Then ask them to turn to card 7 (all groups start on the same card). Every 5–10 minutes after that, tell each group the number of their next news report card. When the time is complete, put the newspapers on the wall for students to look at.

Activity card numbers:
3   4   11   12   15   16   17   21   23   25   30   31   32

Captions for Unit 15

Exercise 2 (page 54)

These are the captions that accompanied the photographs originally:

a) **We are the champions…Pakistan supporters in Southall, west London, reach a frenzy of excitement as World Cup Victory draws nearer.**

b) **Spelling it out…Construction workers Jim Corbett and Richard Anderson prepare to replace the lettering on Brighton's 123-year-old West Pier after restoration.**

c) **Slow breeder…lab technician Joyce Ellis with a partula tohiveana snail, part of Nottingham University's breeding programme, which has seen worldwide numbers increase from four to 300.**

d) **Looming problems…new machinery in the UK, but no new jobs.**

e) **Keeping a secret…Annie Clarke, this year's president, with daughter Mitzi Hayhurst, chief pudding maker, by the boiling dish.**
   (Every 21 years, the village of Great Aughton, Lancashire makes a gigantic pudding, weighing over 2,500kg.)

Letterheads for Unit 12

Distant Horizons

68 Glover Street, Bristol BS6 7HU   Tel 0272 897452   Fax 0272 897464

Traveller's World

67 LYMINGTON ROAD LONDON SW4 6GT
TEL 081-786 1897   FAX 081-786 4444

Mastheads for Unit 16

The CITIZEN

THE POST

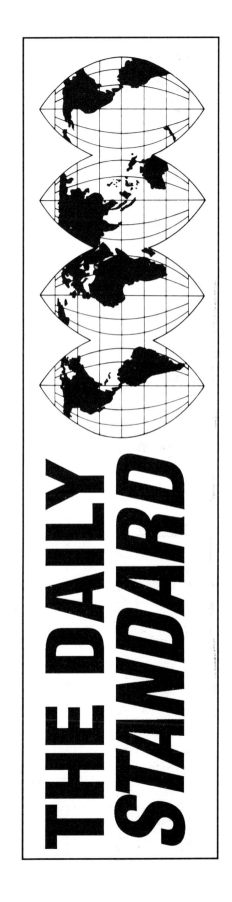

Acknowledgements

The author and publishers are grateful to the authors and others who have given permission for the use of copyright material identified in the text. It has not been possible to identify the sources of all the material used and in some cases the publishers would welcome information from copyright owners.

on p. 3: photographs on top left and bottom right by Andrew Littlejohn, centre top and centre bottom by Bill Godfrey, top right and bottom left by Jeremy Pembrey; on p. 11: John McFarland/Science Photo Library for the photograph of an antechamber to an operating theatre, Trevor Richard/Robert Harding Picture Library for the 'Buttercup yellow drawing room', Leslie Garland Picture Library for the room in Jakarta, William Mason/Ingrid Mason Pictures for the Swedish room, Andrew Littlejohn for the Japanese room, on p. 12: Timothy Woodcock Photolibrary for the cottage window in Ardare, Ireland, Leslie Garland Picture Library for the photograph of housing in Happy Valley, Hong Kong, Robert Harding Picture Library for the window of the Mir's Palace, Pakistan and for the window in Beaucaire, France; Penguin Books Ltd for the haiku by Matsio Basho on p. 19 from *The Penguin Book of Japanese Verse* (p. lxvi), translated with an introduction by Geoffrey Bownas and Anthony Thwaite (Penguin Books, 1964) translation and introduction copyright © Geoffrey Bownas and Anthony Thwaite 1964, and Kakimori Bunko, Hyogo-Ken, Japan for the text of the haiku in Japanese; Carcanet Press Ltd for the extract from 'The Regrets' on p. 19 from *Selected Poems* by C. H. Sisson; Peters Fraser & Dunlop for 'Two Haiku' on p. 19 from *Waving at Trains* by Roger McGough, published by Random Century; Jonathan Cape Ltd and Leonard Cohen Stranger Music Inc. for 'Summer Haiku' on p. 19 from *The Spice-Box of the Earth* by Leonard Cohen, copyright © 1961 Leonard Cohen Stranger Music Inc., used by permission, all rights reserved; HarperCollins Publishers, New York, for the poem on p. 21 'Days that the wind takes over' from *The Window Tree* by Karla Kuskin, copyright © 1975 by Karla Kuskin; George Allen & Unwin, now Unwin Hyman of HarperCollins Publishers Ltd for the poem on p. 22 'Lazy man's song' by Arthur Waley from *Translations from the Chinese*; 'Leisure' by W. H. Davies on p. 22 is from *The Complete Poems of W. H. Davies* published by Jonathan Cape; Brittany Ferries for the extract on p. 28 from *Sailings and Fares, France and Spain*; InterCity for the extract on p. 28 from *A Guide to Services*; photograph of a notice on p. 28 by Andrew Littlejohn; Science Research Associates Ltd for the material on pp. 30–33 from the CoRT Thinking Programme by Edward de Bono (Science Research Associates Ltd, Newtown Road, Henley-on-Thames, Oxfordshire RG9 1EW, Tel. 0491-410111); on p. 44: photograph of a beach in Bali by Andrew Littlejohn; photograph of New Zealand in winter by Pictor International; pp. 47–8: The Spanish National Tourist Office for the advertisement, Ford Motor Company Ltd for the advertisement for the Ford Scorpio © Ford Motor Company Ltd; Explore Worldwide for the advertisement, K Shoes for the advertisement for trainers; p. 49: Jeremy Pembrey for the photographs; *The Guardian* for the following articles on p. 53: 'Gas chief receives second big rise' by Simon Beavis, 'Hoot provokes assault', and 'Channel ferries lose money'; Express Newspapers plc for the article on p. 53 '£5 insult after baby eats glass' from the *Daily Express*; Syndication International Ltd for the article on p. 53 'Fifty flee in rail crash fire scare'; p. 54: Greg Jenson/Associated Press for the car overturned by a tornado, David Sillitoe/*The Guardian* for the Pakistan supporters, Roger Bamber for the letter from Brighton Pier, John Robertson for the snail; p. 55: Don McPhee/*The Guardian* for the woman at a loom; Denis Thorpe/*The Guardian* for the women in the boiling dish.

Drawings by Chris Evans and Helena Green.
Text artwork by James Ducker, Peter Ducker and Wenham Arts.
Book designed by Peter Ducker MSTD.